£3.99

3

Theodore Bayley Hardy

VC DSO MC

To Chad
Happy Birthday

An example of cold bravery....

Theodore Bayley Hardy
VC DSO MC

David Raw

Pen & Sword
MILITARY

First published in Great Britain in 2018 by
Pen & Sword Military
An imprint of
Pen & Sword Books Ltd
Yorkshire – Philadelphia

ISBN 978 1 47382 322 8

A CIP catalogue record for this book is available from the British Library.

Printed and bound in England by TJ International, Padstow, PL28 8RW

Pen & Sword Books Limited incorporates the imprints of Atlas, Archaeology, Aviation, Discovery, Family History, Fiction, History, Maritime, Military, Military Classics, Politics, Select, Transport, True Crime, Air World, Frontline Publishing, Leo Cooper, Remember When, Seaforth Publishing, The Praetorian Press, Wharncliffe Local History, Wharncliffe Transport, Wharncliffe True Crime and White Owl.

For a complete list of Pen & Sword titles please contact

PEN & SWORD BOOKS LIMITED
47 Church Street, Barnsley, South Yorkshire, S70 2AS, England
E-mail: enquiries@pen-and-sword.co.uk
Website: www.pen-and-sword.co.uk

Or

PEN AND SWORD BOOKS
1950 Lawrence Rd, Havertown, PA 19083, USA
E-mail: Uspen-and-sword@casematepublishers.com
Website: www.penandswordbooks.com

Contents

Introduction and Acknowledgements   vii
'It's Only Me, Boys'   xi
Taken with a Summons   xiii

Chapter 1   His First Avowed Intent   1

Chapter 2   Teacher   15

Chapter 3   Priest   25

Chapter 4   Bentham and Hutton Roof   29

Chapter 5   To be a Padre   42

Chapter 6   A Meeting with Woodbine Willie   48

Chapter 7   To the Front Line   55

Chapter 8   Over the Top: Arras, April 1917   77

Chapter 9   A Place Called Passchendaele   88

Chapter 10 Waiting for a Boy to Live   101

Chapter 11 For Valour: The Victoria Cross   104

Chapter 12 Mr Valiant-For-Truth   117

Chapter 13 Mr Valiant-For-Truth Crosses the River   132

Notes   144
Index   149

Theodore Bayley Hardy VC DSO MC.

Introduction and Acknowledgements

I first wrote about Theodore Bayley Hardy thirty years ago in a slim volume entitled *It's Only Me* – Hardy's modest and reassuring greeting to the men when he toured the trenches and outposts on the Western Front. It was published on the seventieth anniversary of Hardy's death, in time for a commemorative service in St John's Church, Hutton Roof. This much fuller biography is to mark the centenary of his death.

The casual visitor to Carlisle Cathedral will immediately notice massive sandstone walls, a magnificent ceiling, and the exquisite Flemish carving of the Brougham Triptych on the northern side. Less obvious, close to the Flemish Triptych, is a dark brass memorial plaque in a timber frame.

It commemorates a man who knew Flanders for other reasons – and who would have preferred the plaque not to be noticed. It is to a man who covered his medal ribbons with his arm through embarrassment and disappeared whenever the 'top brass' sought him out. When congratulated by a sergeant on the award of the Victoria Cross he muttered, 'It's all a mistake of the War Office,' and scurried off. He was at one time a schoolmaster and an unassuming, short-sighted, modest country vicar. He was the most decorated non-combatant in the First World War. His decorations were won not in hot blood and anger, but with cool tenacious courage. He was to die of wounds only a few days before the Armistice.

My first knowledge of Theodore Bayley Hardy was a casual sight of the memorial plaque. It set off an urge to know more about a by then forgotten hero and led to the writing of that first brief biography entitled *It's Only Me*.

Over the years I have come across much new material and information which sheds more light on Hardy's character, motivation, and beliefs as well as his family background and the friends and events which influenced him. The centenary of his death seems an appropriate time to rewrite and add much to that original slim biography.

Hardy's story is one of incredible heroism which should never be forgotten. In today's world, where selfishness and individual greed appear to dominate, it is a story of comradeship and unselfishness which ought to give pause for thought. Above all, it is one man's Christian witness which even the most sceptical agnostic or strident atheist must respect.

One of the delights when writing the original biography was to meet people who had personal connections with Theodore Hardy. Sadly, many of them are no longer with us.

I remember with particular gratitude and affection his granddaughter Patricia Hastings Hardy for her kind hospitality, enthusiasm and help in providing original material and family information. It was a delight to be with Patricia when we discovered the German pillbox on the edge of Rossignol Wood where her grandfather performed one of the deeds that led to his Victoria Cross.

A great debt is also owed to the late Canon Michael Westropp of Kirkby Lonsdale for his support and encouragement. Michael introduced me to Patricia and very generously agreed to underwrite the publication costs to the publishers. Fortunately this generosity never needed to be called on.

It was also a great pleasure to meet and interview the then 90-year-old ex-Private Jimmy Watson who served with the 8th Lincolns in Theodore Hardy's time. Jimmy had very fond memories of Captain Hardy. As a stretcher bearer he helped to carry in his mortally wounded, 'Dear old Padre'. It was Jimmy who first told me of Hardy's catch phrase, 'It's only me, boys'. Later, to stand on the bridge at Briastre with Jimmy and Patricia arm in arm was a never to be forgotten experience – enhanced by the local farmer who firmly nailed Patricia's poppy cross to the bullet scarred wall of his barn next to the bridge. It was still there when last I visited.

A debt is owed to someone I never met: Hardy's sister-in-law, Mary Hardy, wife of his older brother Ernest. Mary published a memoir, *Hardy V.C.*, in 1920. It included extracts from letters sent to her from officers and men who had served with him in the two battalions that together came under his pastoral care, the 8th Lincolns and 8th Somerset Light Infantry. It helped to provide a central core of source material. I was given a copy by Patricia, made even more interesting because it contained sometimes sharp and acerbic written annotations by Hardy's daughter Elizabeth in the margins.

Theodore Hardy always carried a standard issue Chaplains' Department pocket Bible with him. It is the small bulge to be seen in his breast pocket just below his medal ribbons in his studio portrait. His many annotations and markings give a fascinating insight into Hardy's thoughts and faith. I am extremely grateful to the Right Reverend George Hacker, former Bishop of Penrith, for analysing it and assisting me with a theological commentary. Bishop George has been helpful in so many other ways and I thank him and his wife June for their kindness. The pocket Bible was safely deposited in the archives of the Royal Army Chaplains' Department near Andover by Patricia.

Thanks are due to the Regimental Museums of both the Lincolnshire Regiment and the Somerset Light Infantry, and to the Somerset Archive Office. David Blake, curator of the Royal Army Chaplains' Department has become a helpful friend giving me an insight into the history of the Department and the use of the archive.

I am also indebted to Simon Williams, Head of History, and Yvette Gunther, Head Librarian and archivist at Nottingham High School for their very enthusiastic support in trawling through their archives and for giving me permission to use much new material. Hardy's portrait hangs in the school entrance hall, and it was a real thrill to stand in his original classroom. Thanks are also due to Terry Heard, archivist at City of London School.

In Hutton Roof, a very special thank you for all her help is due to Ann Huntington, Church Warden of St John the Divine Church and village post mistress for more than forty years. Richard and Annabel Challenor welcomed me to the old Vicarage. Ann, Annabel and Richard were my companions when, with Patricia Hastings Hardy, we toured the battlefields in Hardy's footsteps, laying wreathes from the village on his grave and in Rossignol Wood.

Steve Wright and Mary Gardiner were very welcoming and helpful in finding material about the curate Hardy at Burton Joyce in the last years of the nineteenth century. It was a great experience to see the familiar TBH signature in the Parish Register for his very first baptism.

I also thank the Imperial War Museum for permission to reproduce photographs held in their collection and to the various authors and their publishers who have allowed me to quote from their works.

Mary Hardy hoped that one day a fuller account would be written of her brother in-law's exploits. I hope this book will to some extent answer that hope and that she would have been pleased with it. I do so wish Patricia could have shared it.

A big thank you is due to Charles, Kate, Heather and their team at Pen & Sword in Barnsley… and to Sue for putting up with an untidy study, a hogging of the computer and endless conversations beginning with 'Do you know ?' and 'Did I tell you ?' – to which the answer was usually 'Yes'.

I would like to thank all who have given permission to use their copyrighted material. Attempts have been made to contact the owners of all copyrighted material, and if anyone's copyright has been inadvertently infringed, I hope my sincere apologies will be accepted. Every effort has been made to check for mistakes in the text, but for any mistakes that remain, they are entirely my own.

Finally, a word of apology to T.B.H. I'm certain, dear Padre, you would not have liked or wished to have been written about. You would probably have scurried off somewhere out of sight. Well, I'm sorry, but I'm afraid your witness, example and selflessness should be shared as an example to all in this the year of your centenary. Please understand and forgive.

David Raw, Dunbar, 2018.

'It's Only Me, Boys'

After this it was noised abroad that Mr. Valiant-for-truth was taken with a summons by the same post as the other, and had this for a token that the summons was true, that his pitcher was broken at the fountain. When he understood it he called for his friends, and told them of it. Then said he, I am going to my Father's; and though with great difficulty I am got hither, yet now I do not repent me of all the trouble I have been at to arrive where I am. My sword I give to him that shall succeed me in my pilgrimage, and my courage and skill to him that can get it. My marks and scars I carry with me, to be a witness for me that I have fought His battles who now will be my rewarder.

When the day that he must go hence was come, many accompanied him to the river side, into which as he went he said, 'Death, where is thy sting?' And as he went down deeper, he said, 'Grave, where is thy victory?' So he passed over, and all the trumpets sounded for him on the other side.

Mr Valiant-for-Truth crosses the river
Pilgrim's Progress
John Bunyan

This posthumous portrait shows Hardy wearing his medal ribbons with a wound stripe on his left arm and the Golden Horseshoe badge of the 37th Division on his shoulder. It now hangs in the Royal Army Chaplains' Department at Andover.

Portrait of Captain the Reverend Theodore Bayley Hardy vc dso mc cf, Chaplain to King George V, by Howard Somerville.

Taken with a Summons

5.00 am, 11 October 1918, River Selle, Briastre.

They knew he would come. He always did. Every night, you could count on it. Sometimes he came from in front of them, from no man's land. He'd even been shot at by some of them when their nerves were twitching.

Sometimes he brought a wounded man on his back, sometimes a body. 'It's only me, boys,' he would say. 'There's nothing to be afraid of. He won't hurt you. Help me to bury him and then I'll read the Burial Service. You can join in if you wish.'

Tonight, though, he had come from behind them with a team of Lewis Gunners and stretcher bearers. He had scrambled down the bank and crossed the plank bridge just finished by the Engineers over the River Selle. All he brought tonight was cigarettes and the comfort of his presence.

He didn't need to say much. It was enough just to be with them. He asked if they had any letters he could take back. They spoke in whispers because the enemy was close. It couldn't last much longer, they said. They had advanced thirty miles in the last month. Could the next Christmas be the first one of peace after over four years?

A few birds sounded the coming dawn. 'I have to go', he said. Minutes later they heard a shot as he crossed the bridge. Seventy years later, Jimmy Watson could still remember him saying, 'I've been hit. I'm sorry to be a nuisance.' Machine-gun fire broke out all around the bridge and the advance platoons.

It was 11 October 1918, exactly a month before the Armistice. The 8th Lincolns and 8th Somersets saw only eight more days of action. A week later, their padre, Theodore Bayley Hardy VC DSO MC, died of his wounds in Number Two British Red Cross Hospital, Rouen. His daughter Elizabeth, herself a Red Cross nurse, wrote to thank the stretcher bearers for bringing him in when under fire.

'Yes', they wrote back, 'it was difficult, but we would go through Hell itself for our dear old Padre.'

Chapter One

His First Avowed Intent

On 20 October 1863 a son was born to George and Sarah Richards Hardy in the Southernhay district of Exeter. He was christened Theodore Bayley Hardy.

Southernhay was, and still is, a pleasant area of Exeter close to the Cathedral just outside the old city walls. In the late eighteenth century speculative developers had built terraces of fine town houses for the well to do. There is an air of respectability to Southernhay.

The new baby was born into a large family. His mother, Sarah, was previously married to Henry Huntley, a dental surgeon in Barnfield Place, Exeter. She had three children from this marriage – Henry, Georgina and Hubert – but was widowed at the early age of 29 in 1855. In 1859, four years later, she married 38-year-old George Hardy. Four more sons were born, Alfred, Ernest, Theodore and the youngest, Robert.[1]

Exeter Cathedral, close to Hardy's birthplace.

George Hardy too had been previously married (in 1849 to Elizabeth Wilkinson) and been widowed (sadly, Elizabeth died in 1853 at the age of just 29). Elizabeth's father, William John Playter Wilkinson was a man of some local significance as Mayor of Exeter in 1837 and was a prosperous wine and spirit merchant.

George Hardy was a commercial traveller. At different times he represented firms in the textile industry from as far away as Leeds, Manchester and Stroud. Later, and as it turned out, significantly, he was employed as a traveller in the wine and spirit trade by his first father-in-law, William Wilkinson. No doubt utilising the recently developed railway system, he was frequently away from home.

The life of a commercial traveller promised great rewards to the successful, but it was also difficult and stressful. George Moore, the Victorian merchant and philanthropist had started life as a commercial traveller. He went on to make a fortune, become a friend of Charles Dickens, and the subject of a biography by Samuel Smiles. He was a generous donor to many charities, hospitals and Schools. In particular he founded the Commercial Traveller Schools which later would have a significant part in the life of the young Theodore Bayley Hardy. Moore gave a sympathetic description of the life of commercial travellers such as George Hardy: 'They were the companions of my early struggles. I have always sympathised with them. I know the risks which they run, the temptations to which they are exposed, and the sufferings which they have to undergo. They spend most of their time away from their homes and families. They are exposed to every change in the weather from the heat of the summer to the storms of the winter. They are liable to be cut off by bronchitis and lung diseases.'[2]

The growing Hardy family's happiness and security was short lived. George Hardy died on 13 October 1870, just a week before Theodore's seventh birthday. The death certificate reveals that George died of long standing heart failure and liver failure associated with alcohol. He must have sampled too many of his samples.[3]

A side effect of liver failure is a build-up of toxins in the brain leading to hepatic encephalopathy which causes confusion, hallucinations, personality change and ultimately coma. For the last few months of his life, George Hardy was confined to Wonford House Hospital in Exeter, which until 1869 carried the name of St Thomas' Hospital for Lunatics.[4]

The death of his father must have had a devastating and profound effect on the 6-year-old Theodore. His father's funeral took place close to his seventh birthday which would normally have been a joyful occasion. The most obvious consequence was that Theodore became a lifelong teetotaller.

Modern research into the effects on children of having an alcoholic parent indicates certain general character traits. This is especially so in what are classed as 'the resilient children of alcoholics', a description strongly applying to Theodore Hardy.

Many such children enter the caring professions such as nursing or teaching. They have a strong drive to help 'save' others whom they regard as weak or in danger. They often blame themselves for failing to 'save' an alcoholic parent leading to a strong adult drive to 'save' others who are in any way vulnerable. They are reluctant to condemn others but often judge themselves harshly, deprecating their own successes and achievements. They have an over-developed sense of responsibility and develop defence mechanisms to protect themselves from too much psychological pain. They can often be solitary and tend to avoid authority figures. They are uncomfortable with praise and recoil from those they regard as punitive. For those with religious belief they look to a God as a forgiving rather than a punitive Father. Indeed they often hope that God will save the errant parent in a life after death. For boys, the deprivation of a father figure sometimes leads to a need to take advice and to find trust in an older substitute father figure.[5]

Readers must judge for themselves whether, and how far, these character traits can be seen in the adult Theodore Bayley Hardy. It is known that he had difficulty with the damnatory clauses of the Athanasian Creed. His refusal to say it delayed his eventual ordination into the priesthood. His older brother Ernest, to whom he always stayed close for the rest of his life, was also ordained after an earlier career as a teacher and had the same difficulties.

George Hardy's death, at a time when there was no welfare state, profoundly affected the financial circumstances of his widow and six children. Prudently, George had contributed for nine years to the Merchants & Travellers Insurance Association which eventually provided an education for Theodore and his brothers. Fortunately, Theodore's mother was an able and enterprising woman. In Morris's Directory of Devonshire for 1870 she is listed as having 'a select preparatory school for young gentlemen'.

Theodore's half-sister, 20-year-old Georgina Huntley, assisted as 'a day governess', or what would now be called a child minder.[6] The income from teaching helped Sarah to survive financially when George was forced to give up work, and later when she was a widow. It allowed a more comfortable existence and enabled them to remain in a respectable part of the city. Theodore's future sister-in-law, Mary Hardy, remembered a large early Victorian house with tall windows and shallow staircases. It was to become the Exeter YMCA, and later was converted in to an estate agent's office. It now bears a green plaque commemorating it as the birthplace of the Reverend Theodore Bayley Hardy VC DSO MC.

At first after their father's death, Theodore and Ernest stayed at home and were taught by their mother. Two years later, in 1872, they were both granted free places at the Royal Commercial Travellers School in Pinner. The school governors' records show that Theodore, aged 9, was admitted at the third time of asking. The school admission book records the family's financial circumstances: 'Four boys unprovided for; under their mother's care who supports them and herself by keeping a small school, which brings in about £35 yearly.'[7]

The origins of the Royal Commercial Travellers School were fairly recent. In 1841 Robert Cuffley, a successful commercial traveller, inaugurated a mutual welfare organisation, the Merchants & Travellers Insurance Association.

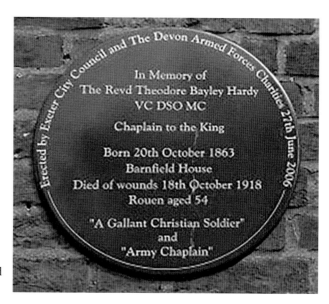

Green plaque at Barnfield House.

Cuffley negotiated an arrangement whereby one sixteenth of any profits of the Association would be set aside for founding a school for children whose fathers had died or were seriously handicapped as a result of their work as commercial travellers. George Hardy had become a member of the Association in 1861.

John Robert Cuffley, founder of the Royal Commercial Travellers School.

The school was a classic example of Victorian charity and 'self-help'. It opened in 1845 as The Commercial Travellers School for Orphan and Necessitous Children. It was unusual for its time in that it catered for both boys and girls and had no denominational test of admission. A history of the school describes a school, 'which would house, feed, clothe and educate the necessitous children of brethren "on the road" who met untimely death or became unable to earn their livelihood'.

Amongst the subscribers were the already mentioned George Moore, and his friend Charles Dickens, who was himself an orphan and the author of *Oliver Twist*, written seven years earlier.[8]

The Commercial Travellers School, Pinner.

By 1855 the school had grown to well over three hundred children, (many, like the Hardy brothers were boarders). It was established in a new handsome Victorian Gothic building formally opened by Albert, the Prince Consort. Land in Pinner had been purchased at an advantageous price from the London & North Western Railway Company close to the West Coast main line.

By the standards of the day, the school reflected the enlightened progressive liberal values of its founders – Dickens no doubt ensured there was to be no Thomas Gradgrind on the staff. The school offered a radical broad curriculum; it included science, mathematics, book-keeping, geography, history, art, poetry, music, and handicrafts as well as the classics. It had a generous eighteen acres of playing fields where Theodore, despite his short sight, learned to love cricket and kept fit riding a bicycle. He also learned to swim and began a lifetime habit of starting the day with a cold bath.

The school finally closed in 1967 for financial reasons, but the building still stands and contains a memorial plaque to the Reverend Theodore Bayley Hardy VC DSO MC. It is maintained by The Mercurians, an old scholars' association.

The two Hardy brothers did well academically, although it was Theodore who won the prizes. Ernest left in 1878, securing a post for four years as a tutor in a small boarding preparatory school owned by a Mrs Oliver in Park Crescent, Worthing.[9] He later went on to Queen's University, Belfast before being ordained in the Church of England. It was in Belfast that Ernest met and married his wife Mary. He eventually became Vicar of Thetford in Norfolk. Mary Hardy was to produce a small limited edition memoir to her brother-in-law, *Hardy V.C.*, shortly after the Great War.[10]

The Commercial Travellers School had close associations with the City of London School (in Milk Street off Cheapside in the heart of the City). The relationship included the provision of scholarships for able boys. Theodore's academic achievements led to the award of a full scholarship of three pounds ten shillings (plus books) per term to attend the City of London School.[11]

Hardy was not the first young orphan to be educated there. A future Prime Minister, Herbert Asquith, orphaned by the loss of his father at the age of seven, preceded Theodore by ten years. Asquith was supremely intelligent, winning all the prizes at Balliol College, Oxford. Asquith was caricatured as 'Brains' in *Vanity Fair*, went on to serve as Gladstone's Home Secretary in the 1890s and later becoming a successful reforming peacetime Prime Minister, laying the foundations of the welfare state. He was Prime Minister when Great Britain entered the war in 1914, until December 1916.

Unlike the Travellers School, City of London had no boarding facilities and Theodore attended as a day boy. His mother Sarah sold up in Exeter and purchased an Annuity with the proceeds. She moved to London to 124 Elgin Road in the Paddington/Marylebone area to provide a home for Theodore. Theodore's half-brother, Hubert Huntley, joined them from Exeter and contributed to the household income by working as a draper's clerk. The resourceful Sarah also rented out a room to a young stockbroker's clerk, and they had sufficient income to employ a live in housemaid.[12]

Theodore entered the City of London School in January 1879 at the relatively old age for a new entrant of 15. He spent three and a half years there and it had a profound effect on him. He made life-long friendships and the boy became a man. City of London School could trace its origins back to 1442 as a charitable institution for 'four poor boys', but its rise to prominence was comparatively recent. In 1825, a group of radical reformers, progressive educationalists, slave abolitionists, Quakers, non-conformists, and the Jewish community, led by Henry Brougham and George Birkbeck, established University College, later to become London University. The new University was a radical response to Oxford and Cambridge, and later to Durham, where the Church of England had a religious test entry bar. The group then decided to create a permanent school out of excess charitable funds from the old 1442 school foundation. In 1834 Brougham, by now Lord Chancellor in the Whig Government, drove through the necessary Act of Parliament to enable the Corporation of London to take over the charitable foundation and to establish a School Committee as the new governing body. The committee was administered by the City Corporation.

Brougham laid the foundation stone of the new building in Milk Street in the heart of the City. The school opened its doors to 400 boys in 1837. At the foundation stone dinner, Brougham declared the radical liberal background to the school. 'Dissenters of every shade – Protestant and Catholic – Jew and Gentile – all will be admitted to the same advantages; religious instruction will be imparted under the eye of their parents – in the bosom of their families; and by the pastors approved by their parents.'[13]

Brougham's group held what were then regarded as revolutionary ideas. London University had no denominational admission tests, unlike the ancient Universities at Oxford and Cambridge which admitted only members of the established Anglican Church. Similarly, the new City of London School had no religious tests for either boys or masters and it became a beacon of religious toleration. Nevertheless the school had, and still has, a strong musical tradition with the Choir linked to the Chapel Royal.

City of London School, Milk Street, off Cheapside.

The curriculum was wide-ranging and broke away from the monopoly of the classics which dominated the established public schools. It included provision for English, Latin, French, Greek (plus optional German, Hebrew, Spanish and Italian), arithmetic, mathematics and natural philosophy, geography and natural history, ancient and modern history, choral singing, chemistry and other branches of experimental philosophy, logic and ethics. The Reverend Doctor Mortimer (Headmaster 1840–65), a campaigner against the slave trade in his youth, introduced a Debating Society. The school throbbed with new ideas and a school magazine to be run by the boys was established.[14]

The School quickly gained a reputation for achievement, producing a whole series of distinguished mathematicians, scientists and engineers. One of them, the marine engineer Henry Beaufoy, set up a series of generous scholarships. The young Theodore Bayley Hardy was a beneficiary of a Beaufoy scholarship.

In 1867 the Government appointed the Taunton Commission to report measures for the improvement of secondary education. The Commission noted that the science based curriculum helped to integrate a wide social intake. They pronounced that City of London School was 'by far the best among the secondary schools of London'. The success of the school was part of the pressure that lead up to the Universities Tests Act (1870) by the Gladstone government. The act abolished religious admission tests at Oxford, Cambridge and Durham.

As mentioned, one of the school's old boys, regarded then as its most distinguished and gifted, was the future Prime Minister, Herbert Asquith. Asquith, a Congregationalist, took advantage of Gladstone's abolition of the religious admission tests to Oxford in the autumn of 1870, at the age of 17. As Gladstone's Home Secretary in the 1890s, he spoke at an old boys' dinner in 1895 and remembered, 'the stimulating environment in Milk Street with the sound of Bow Bells and the roar of traffic in Cheapside. I think of the daily walk through the crowded, noisy, jostling streets; I think of the river with its barges and its steamers, and its manifold active life; I think of St Paul's Cathedral and Westminster Abbey, and of the National Gallery.[15]

Hardy arrived at City of London in January 1879 and was placed into the 4th class. He soon settled and was promoted to the 5th class in the summer. He quickly succeeded, winning the Classical Progress Prize in his second term and the Mathematical Proficiency Prize a year later before entering the sixth form. He made a number of close friends who remained in touch with him for the rest of his life. If one judges a person's character by the friends they keep, then Theodore's friends shed light on who he was and what he believed.

One close friend was Charles Heath – captain of school, captain of sports and a rowing companion of Hardy. Heath went on to be an outstanding scholar at St John's College, Cambridge. Like Hardy he was ordained. He became Senior Master at King Edward's School, Birmingham. After the war Heath wrote of his friend, 'I feel proud to have been fond of T.B. Hardy, with whom I sat in Durham's science lecture in the theatre and often walked up Cheapside after school.'[16]

Hardy was much more than just a hard working student. He had quiet authority and was well liked and respected by his fellows. He was elected captain of the Beaufoy Rowing Club in his last term. The club secretary was another close friend, Charles Edward Montague (1867–1928).

The school magazine of April 1882 records, 'on Friday, March 17th, a meeting of the Beaufoy Rowing Club was held in the sixth form room, Mr Moses in the chair. After receiving the Secretary's report for last year, the election of officers was at once proceeded with. The result was as follows:

Charles Edward Montague
(1867–1928).

Captain, Mr T.B. Hardy; Vice-Captain, Mr E. C. Slade-Jones; Secretary, Mr
C.E. Montague. The club at present numbers nearly twice as many members
as it did last year, and a pleasant season is expected.'[17]

In a 1965 history of City of London School, A.E. Douglas-Smith wrote,
'The Beaufoy Rowing Club attracted many of the School's finest sons; but none
were more true to her finest traditions than T.B. Hardy and C.E. Montague.'[18]
Charles Montague was a close friend of Hardy at City of London School.
He came from a Catholic Irish family (his father having abandoned the
priesthood in order to marry). He achieved fame as a distinguished novelist,
author and playwright and became deputy editor of the liberal newspaper
the *Manchester Guardian*. When the *Guardian*'s editor C.P. Scott was elected
to parliament as a Liberal MP, Montague was acting as editor (having
previously married Scott's daughter). Their son, Aubrey, featured as one of
the actors playing the British Olympic athletes in the film *Chariots of Fire*.

Like Hardy, Montague served with distinction in the Great War. In August
1914 he was opposed to the declaration of war on principle. Yet once war

started he believed there was no going back and it was right to support the war effort in the hope of a swift resolution. In 1914 he was 47, well over the age for enlistment. To be enlisted, he dyed his white hair black, gave a false age to the authorities, and joined the 24th Royal Fusiliers as a private soldier. He later accepted a commission in Military Intelligence at MI7 as an official press censor and writer of propaganda. He was promoted again to be an intelligence officer on Haig's staff escorting VIPs including Lloyd George and Clemenceau on tours of the front. Henry Nevinson, war correspondent and joint founder of the Friends Ambulance Unit wrote, 'Montague is the only man I know whose white hair in a single night turned dark through courage.'[19]

After the war, Montague returned to writing and the *Manchester Guardian*. In 1922 he published a deeply critical book, *Disenchantment*, on the conduct of the war and its causes. It is still in print today. The chapter 'The Sheep That Were Not Fed' is a highly critical account of the role of army chaplains. There was though an exception, his old friend. 'There was the hero and saint, T.B. Hardy, to whom a consuming passion of human brotherhood brought, as well as rarer things, the MC, the DSO, the VC, the unaccepted invitation of the King to come home as one of his own chaplains and live, and then the death which everyone had seen to be certain'.[20]

Another profound influence on the young Hardy was his dynamic, charismatic headmaster, Dr Edwin Abbott. Abbott was an old boy of the school and a scholar of the first rank. At St John's, Cambridge he took the highest honours in the classical, mathematical and theological tripos. He was ordained in 1862 and taught at King Edward School, Birmingham. He was appointed Head of City of London School in 1865 at the youthful age of 26. He was just 40 when Theodore Hardy arrived from Pinner.

Dr Edwin Abbott (1838–1926).
Headmaster, City of London School.

Abbott was a man of immense energy and intellect, known for his liberal inclinations in theology, his educational views and his books, some of which are still in print today. He was the father figure Hardy never had.[21]

Hardy's friend Charles Heath recorded, 'Of Abbott, no pupil of his could ever say enough in praise. "The Doctor" was perhaps something of a terror to boys in the lower parts of the School, but you no sooner came under his influence in the classroom and survived the tremendous energy of his stimulus than you became a hero-worshipper for life. He was perhaps the greatest teacher there ever was, the most inspiring counsellor, and the very kindest and most understanding of friends. Considering the shortcomings of the elder part of his staff, the success of the school at the universities is almost incredible. An example of his method was his annual viva-voce examination of each individual class (below the Latin class, I think) during a week in December when the Sixth were reading six books of the Iliad in their homes! All his lessons were memorable, but he was perhaps at his greatest in his Greek Testament, his Thucydides, and his English Literature lessons.'[22]

As Theodore Hardy grew to manhood, his sister-in-law tells us that 'London's boundless possibilities for happiness, or unhappiness, oppressed him'. She tells how, for him, music had 'a strange analogy to certain facts in our spiritual life. He found himself led into deep places by the world of sound.' It was his habit to walk to attend the afternoon service in Westminster Abbey every Sunday.[23]

Theodore Hardy left school in the summer of 1882 aged 18. As he was to show time and again later, he had dogged determination and wished to continue his education despite lacking the financial resources to be a full-time student. His solution was to obtain a teaching post in Notting Hill and enrol at London University as an external student for an arts degree. It took six years of part-time study to complete it. He matriculated in June 1883 after a course of private preparatory studies. He was awarded an Intermediate Arts degree in 1887 and a BA with Honours in 1889 (placed 83rd).[24]

Ernest meanwhile had entered Queens University, Belfast on a similar basis. Like Theodore, in time he was ordained a priest in the Church of England. Whenever he could, Theodore visited his brother in Belfast. Both brothers were to have Irish brides.

Ernest's future wife, Mary, remembered seeing Theodore for the first time at a dance in Belfast at the age of 21. 'He was a man with the head of a scholar and the eyes of a poet. I remember being asked, "Who is that distinguished looking young man standing in the corner?"[25]

At such an occasion the young Hardy met Florence Elizabeth Hastings, a friend of his future sister-in-law. It was a love match. She dazzled him and in return, needed his quiet calm and strength.

Ernest's wife, Mary, described her friend Florence, 'She was a markedly handsome girl, fair and graceful. She flashed about with her striking beauty and her wit in a sort of luminous mist. She was a brilliant talker, with a power of drawing in a scene or a personality in a few swift lines, yet without malice or uncharitableness. She was somewhat unconventional, far from being that curious combination of dullness and energy that the Church of England demands in a parson's wife.'[26]

Florence's father, William Hastings (1814–1892) had been the Surveyor of Works for Belfast City Council and played a major role in the Victorian building boom in the city. He later became a freelance architect. The Hastings were known as a clever and literary family, living in a comfortable house in Craigfernie Terrace to the south west of the city off the Lisburn Road. Theodore and Florence married on 13 September 1888 at the Great Victoria Street Baptist Meeting House. He was 25, she was 26. The Meeting House building had been designed by Florence's father in 1866.

The couple returned to London. Theodore completed his studies in 1889, graduating with Honours as Bachelor of Arts. They lived in rented

Great Victoria Street Baptist Chapel, Belfast.[27]

accommodation in Kensington and a daughter, Elizabeth Mary, was born in 1890.

Having graduated, Hardy was determined to make progress in his teaching career. In 1891, after two years teaching in London, and armed with an excellent reference from Dr Abbott, he applied for the post of Form Master to the Upper Second at Nottingham High School. His application was successful and sixteen happy years followed.

Chapter Two

Teacher

Nottingham High School, like the City of London School, had an ancient foundation which it could trace back to 1513, but it had expanded and developed as a response to the demands of a rapidly changing industrial city. It provided an education for the sons of Nottingham's emerging middle class and, like City of London, it had no religious test of admission. In 1868 the rapid growth led to a move to a handsome new Victorian gothic building on Waverley Mount, just to the north of the city centre, opposite the Arboretum Park. It remains there, much expanded, to this day.

City of London School had roots in progressive radicalism and non–sectarianism.

The Rev Dr James Gow. Headmaster of Nottingham High School.

Nottingham High School in 1900, during Hardy's time as a master.

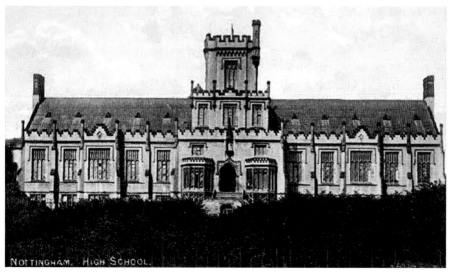

School report signed by Hardy.

Nottingham High School.

OCTOBER, 1892.

Monthly Report of _____ R. Wood

English Subjects _ Very good (specially – Geography) – 1st

Classics _ Very good – 1st

Modern Languages _ Very good – 1st

Mathematics _____

Science _____

Times Detained _____ —   Times Absent _____ —

Excuses for Lessons _____ —   Conduct _ Very good

Signed _ T.B. Hardy B.a.

1st of 27, he has worked very well.

The city of Nottingham could claim similar radical roots. In the first half of the nineteenth century Nottingham was a hotbed of radical protest. There were high levels of Luddite activity and frame breaking early in the century when one of Nottinghamshire's most famous sons, Lord Byron, spoke eloquently in the House of Lords against a bill calling for the death penalty for frame-breakers. Later, Chartists agitated for reform in the 1840s. The city elected the only Chartist Member of Parliament when Feargus O'Connor was elected as the city's MP in 1847. A statue of O'Connor was erected by public subscription after his death in the Arboretum Park close to the High School.[1]

There were other parallels between the two schools. City of London thrived under the dynamic leadership of Dr Abbott, just as Nottingham High did under its forceful, forward thinking headmaster, the Reverend Dr James Gow. Abbott and Gow were both appointed at a relatively young age (26 and 30). Both had distinguished prize winning Cambridge academic backgrounds. Both were Fellows at their college (St John's and Trinity) at a very young age.

Abbott and Gow knew each other well and Abbott's testimonial stood Hardy in good stead. Both had a powerful influence on Hardy and it is not too fanciful to regard both as surrogate father figures.

Before Gow was appointed, in December 1884, the high school suffered a period of stagnation and decline. The governors were determined to remedy the situation. The governing body was chaired by the Duke of St Albans, a former Minister in the Gladstone government and Lord Lieutenant of Nottinghamshire. Another governor was the Bishop of Southwell, George Ridding, a former head of Winchester College who was to play a significant role in Hardy's ordination. In a competitive field, the energetic Gow was chosen out of 112 applicants.[2]

Gow had won prizes in both classics and mathematics at Cambridge. He was also a qualified barrister at law which was useful whenever he encountered opposition to his plans. A mark of his success and reputation at Nottingham was that he eventually became headmaster of Westminster School, one of the premier public schools, in 1901.

Dr Gow was impressed by the earnest 28-year-old Hardy who was only nine years his junior. Dr Abbott's testimonial was persuasive, as was the fact that Hardy had won prizes as a pupil in classics and mathematics at City of London. There was much to admire in the determined way he obtained his degree as an external student. Hardy's calm quiet authority must have been impressive at interview. Gow and Hardy took to each other and maintained a friendship for the rest of Hardy's life.

Gow kept a tight personal control on every aspect of the school. He lived close by at 1 Waverley Street, a handsome Victorian villa facing the lake in Arboretum Park. He kept detailed records of the school accounts in ledgers in a meticulous hand. The records included details of the salaries of the seventeen masters.

When Hardy was first appointed in 1891 his salary was £50 per half year. In July of 1892 it increased to £53 6s 8d, still at the lower end of the scale compared to the two most senior masters on £83 6s 8d per half year.[3]

The high school expanded rapidly under Dr Gow's tenure and by 1891 over three hundred boys were on roll. Many were day boys, but a few were boarders (accommodated with the masters and their wives). The school gained a national reputation for excellence and innovation, particularly in the sciences with a state of the art chemistry laboratory; and it attracted pupils from other parts of the country. Gow also encouraged a wider, broad-based intake locally by arranging scholarships through the local School Board. One such boy who was the recipient of a £12 county scholarship was the novelist D.H. Lawrence.

Gow drove forward curricular changes in mathematics, history, geography, classics and English language, introducing business studies in 1890. He had himself published a series of text books in classics, mathematics and English grammar. In 1897, Hardy made himself useful to Dr Gow (earning an additional stipend) by publishing, through Macmillan, *A Key to Dr Gow's Method of* English. According to the school magazine, *The Foreste*, it was 'a very useful book, showing considerable research both in English Literature and modern philology'.[4] Philology can be defined as, 'the study of language in oral and written historical source, literary criticism, and linguistics'.[5]

Hardy taught one of the two sets in the upper second. The school still has detailed archive records showing the cross-curricular areas which he, as a form master, was required to teach. It provides a fascinating glimpse of the range of curricular content and teaching methods in a leading late Victorian school.

The curriculum was laid down by Dr Gow and had to be taught in every form. In 1900 Hardy is shown as the form master for upper second A. The curriculum also reflects Dr Abbott's influence. Hardy was required to teach:

BIBLE
St Luke's Gospel, Maclear, Shilling Book of New Testament, pp 67/96

REPETITION
St Matthew, chapters 6 and 7; Palgrave, Children's Treasury of English Song, First Part; No 86, Tennyson, The Dying Swan; No.77, No.78.

HISTORY
Nelson's Royal History of England 1066 to 1399

GEOGRAPHY
General Physical Features of Scotland and Ireland

ENGLISH
Gow, *A Method of English*, Section II and Section III, Lessons 1 to 8, English Composition, Parsing and Analysis.

FRENCH
Longman's French course, part 1; J.H. Bertenshaw, *First Conversation French Reading Book*, Illustrated (Longmans)

LATIN

Abbott, *Via Latina*, Ex 33 to 48; Grammar, pp 1 to 93, 00,101, 115 to 117, 126 to 136, 141, 142; Gradatim, sections 48, 53, 54, 65, 76.

Earlier, in 1892, the Upper Second curriculum consisted of:

The Children's Treasury of English Song

History between 1603 and 1660

The Geography of Scotland and Ireland

English Analysis of Simple Sentences

French from the Chardenal French Course, Latin (Dr. Abbott's Via Latina)

Arithmetic – Stocks and Shares – Problems of Area and Proportional Parts

Algebra – Factors – Simple Equations – Easy Problems

Geometry Euclid – Examples 1–26[6]

Theodore Hardy, back row, extreme right. Dr James Gow, front row, fourth from right.

In addition to his own form work, Hardy taught a specialist maths set. It was typical of Hardy that if a boy was punished, it had to have a positive outcome. He ensured that in a detention there was always a mathematical puzzle to solve.

In the summer of 1892, Theodore, Florence and Elizabeth left rented accommodation to move into 7 Yew Tree Avenue in Carrington, just off Mansfield Road. The house was one of a pair of red brick villas designed by the prominent Nottingham architect Watson Fothergill in 1881. It was modest with three storeys. It still stands today but is now converted into flats. It is about a mile north of the high school. Although trams went to the city centre along Mansfield Road, Theodore maintained his habit of cycling to work.

It is possible the house may have been purchased with money left by Florence's father who had died earlier in 1892. The family was now sufficiently well off to employ a domestic servant, Mary Donnelly, originally from Belfast and known to Florence.[7]

Close by was the Church of St John the Evangelist. It was here that the Hardy family worshipped and where early in 1893 their baby son, William Hastings Hardy, was christened. William was to benefit from free education at the high school until the Hardys left Nottingham in 1907.

As well as cycling, Theodore Hardy was always keen on physical exercise and games (and as noted, always starting the day with a cold bath). Unfortunately, his keenness was let down by poor eyesight. Although he regularly played cricket for the Masters against the Boys on the school pitch in Mapperley Park, in sixteen years he failed to score a single run!

As he had done as a pupil at City of London School, he regularly attended the school Debating Society meetings often acting as an impartial chairman. Records of the debates still exist in archive copies of the school magazine. On one occasion he intervened in a debate on Jewish immigration, revealing again the liberal nature of his character.[8]

Nottingham High School has an archive of photographs taken in Hardy's time of each year group with their respective masters. The second form photographs reveal a rather serious looking Hardy but there is also evidence of much kindness on an individual basis. His sister-in-law wrote, 'he was quiet and reserved, but was an untiring and inspiring listener. He loved to sing and music led him into deep places.'[9]

The photographs also belie a lively sense of humour. Despite his seemingly shy reserve, his future padre colleague, Geoffrey Studdert Kennedy, recalled, 'He had the power that belongs to saints. I told him some yarns, and we both roared laughing over them.'[10]

Hardy (centre) wears a slightly quizzical, benevolent smile. There is a poignancy to the ancient school photographs in the school archive. The masters and boys sit together below the steps to the school's main entrance. Hardy in gown, square shouldered, with a steady gaze and the hint of a smile, whilst the boys are be-capped and with large white collars. All look directly at

Theodore Bayley Hardy (centre) at Nottingham High School.

the camera. They were not to know that a generation later the school War Memorial would stand where the cameraman stood and that many of their names, including their master's, would be on it.

Theodore Bayley Hardy was not the only one in the photograph to die in the Great War. Over fifty boys taught directly by him perished in that terrible conflict, many others were to be disabled or disfigured, and of course he knew the brothers of many others. It is known he kept in touch with the high school during the war, receiving the school magazine by post. He wrote many letters of condolence trying to offer what comfort he could to the parents of boys he had taught when news came in the magazine that they were casualties. He also wrote to Dr Gow, by now head of Westminster School, when it was reported that Gow's 23-year-old son, Roderick, was lost on HMS *Defence* in the Battle of Jutland in 1916.[11]

For the survivors, there were fond memories. In 1965, local newspaper publicity about Hardy's medals being presented to the Royal Army Chaplains' Department by his 76-year-old daughter, Elizabeth, brought an affectionate response about his old form master from a former pupil, a Mr A.W. Adams.

In a letter to the Nottingham *Guardian Journal*, Mr Adams recalled, 'He was a very friendly type, but he was a shortish man and the last person you would expect to win a VC.'[12]

One of Nottingham's most famous sons, the novelist and poet D.H. Lawrence, attended the high school when Hardy was there. There is no direct evidence from the school records that Lawrence was taught by Hardy, but it is possible he may have taught him at some time because there was an occasional need to cover a colleague's class.

Lawrence's biographer recalls an obsession with death and a strange correspondence between Lawrence and his brother involving skeletons and coffins. Lawrence's obsession, according to one source in the 1960s, led to a clash with T.B. Hardy. In 1965, the aforementioned A.W. Adams wrote to the Nottingham *Guardian Journal* recounting that Hardy once noticed Lawrence not paying attention in a lesson and preoccupied with the contents of his desk. Hardy lifted the desk to discover Lawrence had been playing with a macabre set of toys: miniature skeletons, gibbets and coffins. Lawrence apparently took to his heels and ran off. According to Mr Adams, Lawrence later sought revenge by firing a paper pellet at Hardy's back when the latter was writing on the blackboard. It must be said the school's current librarian and archivist is sceptical about this story.[13]

Lawrence was the first boy from the small coal mining community of Eastwood to win one of the new £12 County Council Scholarships. The high school records show that he performed well at school, being top of his form in 1900 and winning a mathematics prize. Lawrence's school reports, despite the alleged incident with Hardy, describe his diligence and conduct as 'very good'.[14]

There is a further indirect connection between England's most decorated non-combatant and one of its great novelists. Twenty years later, Lawrence was living with his new wife Frieda von Richthofen, cousin of the 'the Red Baron' Manfred von Richthofen. Hardy and his two battalions were down below

Albert Ball VC DSO & two bars, MC.

in the trenches at Arras during 'Bloody April' in 1917 when the Germans had command of the skies. They were frequently attacked by the Red Baron's Jagdstaffel (Jasta) 11 squadron.

Statue of Albert Ball VC DSO MC in the grounds of Nottingham Castle.

There was a further Richthofen/Hardy/Nottingham High School connection. Hardy was not the only winner of all three gallantry medals to be connected to Nottingham High. The Royal Flying Corps ace, Albert Ball, VC, DSO with two bars, MC, was an old boy of the school, although this was after Hardy left. Ball, son of the Lord Mayor of Nottingham Sir Albert Ball, was killed in May 1917. The German authorities claimed that the Red Baron's younger brother, Lothar von Richthofen, shot Ball down – though the evidence is that Ball's SE5 crashed with engine failure.[15]

Hardy's teaching career continued to develop. He moved on to become a third form master in 1902, and in 1905 he was promoted to become joint master of the new modern sixth.

Then in 1907, an advertisement caught his attention for a new headmaster at Bentham Grammar School on the Yorkshire-Lancashire border near Lancaster.

Appendix: Reverend T.B. Hardy and WWI losses at Nottingham High School.

Between 1891and 1907, Theodore Bayley Hardy was a form master and also taught a maths sets. The forty-nine boys listed below were taught by him and died in the First World War. He also taught many of the brothers of those killed. In a school of less than 350 boys he probably knew them all. The list gives an indication of the terrible losses incurred in the war. Those marked by an asterisk are buried in Belgium and France:

Abbot F.W.

Atherley C.E.

Ball O.H.*

Ball W.W.*

Ballamy H.W.*

Black E.C.*

Brett H.S.*

Calvert A.H.

Crofts F.W.*

Cross W.E.*

Cullen W.H.*

Freestone W.H.

Gillott O.C.

Given M.*

Goodall G.P.

Grant D.P.C.*

Herrick J.R.W.

Howard (Haubitz) W.L.

Hutchinson C.D.

Jackson J.E.*

Levy A.H.

Lewin J.W.*

Marshall W.

Mason C.*

Mellard R.B.*

Mellor P.W.

Millar A.L.

Newmarch G.E.S.

Piggin F.P.L.

Pratt N.H.*

Pyatt G.H.

Pyatt R.G.*

Schloss L.E.

Shipstone F.E.*

Simpson J.H.

Stevens A.L.*

Information kindly supplied by Yvonne Gunther (librarian) and Simon Williams (head of history) at Nottingham High School.

Chapter Three

Priest

On 18 December 1898, at the relatively late age of 35, Theodore Hardy was ordained Deacon in the Church of England at Southwell Minster by the Bishop of Southwell, Dr George Ridding. Southwell Diocese was created in 1884 and covered a large mining and industrial area including the whole of the Nottinghamshire coalfield and part of South Yorkshire.

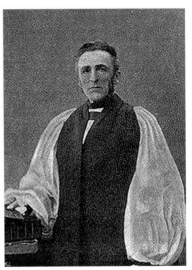

Bishop George Ridding (1828– 1904), first Bishop of Southwell.

Within a year Hardy was ordained as a priest at St George's Church in Nottingham. His brother, Ernest, had already been ordained. It was a step Theodore had contemplated for some ten years. He had held back, according to his sister-in-law Mary, because he was not convinced on some points of Church dogma. He could not accept the damnatory clauses of the Athanasian Creed. It may be this had some deep origin connected to the death of his father. Mary Hardy wrote, 'His oft stated approach was to hate the sin but to forgive the sinner.' He was to demonstrate this throughout his life and it was often remarked upon by several of the officers he had served with in the Great War.[1]

Hardy got to know Bishop Ridding at the High School where the Bishop was a governor. They had much in common and developed a close accord. The Bishop had been a master and later headmaster of Winchester College. He was appointed as the first Bishop of Southwell in 1884 and was known to have progressive liberal views on social and educational matters, often expressing support for the Nottinghamshire miners. According to his biographer, the Bishop was 'A man of conspicuous tact and moderation'.[2] After many discussions with the Bishop, Hardy at last felt able to take the step to ordination.

Also at this time Theodore Hardy first met someone who was also to have a very great influence on him then, and many years later, during the war. The Reverend Llewellyn Gwynne had been recently appointed to the living of Emmanuel Church in the deeply impoverished area of St Ann's in Nottingham.

Gwynne was a burly, charismatic evangelical who had played football for Derby County. He arrived in Nottingham in 1892 and made a massive impact in St Ann's. He modestly claimed to be young, very inexperienced and not very clever, 'but my flock *taught me more than I could teach them*'.[3] Hardy and Gwynne started a coffee tavern and Boys' Club

Bishop Llewellyn Henry Gwynne, CMG CBE (11 June 1863–9 December 1957).

run by the ladies of the Temperance Society, who were also responsible for a Tea Tent on the Forest. Llewellyn Gwynne was a teetotaller all his life and a great supporter of the temperance movement. He also set up open air meetings with choir, clergy and speakers for those parishioners who never came to church.

Apart from football, he was a highly successful amateur cricketer. The two men became friends – a friendship renewed twenty years later when Gwynne, having been Bishop of Khartoum in the Sudan, was appointed to be Deputy Chaplain General (in effect commanding all the padres on the Western Front).[4]

Hardy had great difficulty being accepted as a padre in the first two years of the war because of his age, but it is reasonable to speculate that his old friend intervened on his behalf to enable him to be accepted in 1916.

After his ordination, Hardy was licensed to be curate of St Helen's Church in the village of Burton Joyce, a five-mile bicycle ride to the east of Nottingham.

Burton Joyce today is a prosperous commuter village, but in Hardy's time it was still a village of framework knitters, farm labourers and domestic servants. There was a strong Methodist presence in the village and a living memory of the protest and frame breaking days in the Chartist and Luddite years. Before the arrival of the Reverend Reginald Thompson as vicar in 1884 the established Church had been seen as the focus for the minority of professionals and businessmen.

St Helen's Church, Burton Joyce.

Mr Thompson set to with gusto. He founded an alcohol-free reading room in 1894 with newspapers and books for 'working men'. 'There is a capital billiard table and other games such as chess, draughts and dominoes may also be enjoyed in the recreation room, a smaller room being set aside for reading. It is well furnished and lighted, and the fifty members who now enjoy the use of it are much indebted to Mr Thompson, the vicar, and the other gentlemen who took an active part in the promotion of the little institution.'[5]

To Bishop Ridding, Burton Joyce was an ideal appointment for both Hardy and Mr Thompson's successor as vicar, 70-year-old Reginald Ward. Mr Ward was pleased to get the support of a mature curate in his parish work, but he had much that he could teach the younger man. He was in many ways a sympathetic figure and shared many of Hardy's social and religious views.

Mr Ward was well known for his support and care for the poorer members of society. He encouraged generosity amongst the more prosperous members of the congregation providing practical help with food and clothing. Both men shared an enthusiasm for temperance and Ward had an open, friendly disposition to other denominations. Following a series of child deaths, the Vicar led practical campaigns to improve the health of the village with better drainage and street lighting.

The Vicar started a parish magazine, soon carrying the name of the new curate, Reverend T.B. Hardy BA, on its cover. The magazine contained articles providing practical help and support beyond purely theological matters. Theodore Hardy was welcomed into 'The Harvesters', a cricket team founded and run by the Vicar, though whether Hardy's batting average improved is not known. Bishop Ridding had arranged an ideal training appointment for the new curate. Hardy could learn and contribute and, of personal importance, have a sympathetic father figure with whom he could discuss matters and admire.

Hardy began his curacy assisting at the Christmas services in December 1898. He helped with services on a Sunday whilst continuing to teach at the high school during the week. He conducted his first christening at Whitsuntide on 31 May 1899. The familiar T.B. Hardy signature can still be seen in the Parish Register. He baptised Ernest Archibald Gilbert Holmes, son of Arthur Holmes, master of the local national school, and his wife Gertrude.[6]

| When Baptised. | Child's Christian Name. | Parent's Name. | | Abode. | Quality, Trade, or Profession. | By whom the Ceremony was performed. |
		Christian.	Surname.			
1899 May 31 born Sept 29 1898 No. 1401	Ernest Archibald Gilbert	Arthur and Gertrude Emily	Holmes	Radcliffe-on-Trent	Master in National School	T. B. Hardy
1899 May 31 born April 13 No. 1402	Gladys Watson	Thomas George and Selina Jane	Watson	Cropwell Bishop	Butcher	T. B. Hardy

BAPTISMS solemnized in the Parish of *Burton Joyce cum Bulcote* in the County of *Nottingham* in the Year 1899

Hardy stayed at Burton Joyce for five years until July 1904 when he moved, as curate, to the more conveniently placed St Augustine's Church in New Basford. It was closer to home and the high school. New Basford was a rapidly growing working-class suburb in north Nottingham noted for the manufacture of soap at the Cussons factory and three breweries. It was also a Methodist stronghold. St Augustine's had been built in the late 1870s when Methodists outnumbered Anglicans in the area by a factor of four to one, and relations between Nonconformists and Anglicans had not been good.

The first two years were not easy for Hardy who, despite the convenience of being closer to home, found himself out of sympathy with the Vicar, the Reverend Arthur Dewick. Dewick had objected to inmates of the workhouse being included in his parish in the census for 1901 when they were temporarily living in an old factory on Beech Avenue, while waiting for Bagthorpe Workhouse to be completed. Fortunately Dewick left in 1906.

In 1907 an advertisement caught Hardy's eye. It was a vacancy for a new headmaster at the small Bentham Grammar School located in the far north-west tip of the West Riding of Yorkshire in the Craven district, on the banks of the River Wenning (a tributary of the River Lune) close to the Lancashire border. After consulting Florence and the children, he applied.

Chapter Four

Bentham and Hutton Roof

'He who would valiant be ... 'gainst all disaster.'

The village of Bentham in the old West Riding lies on the western edge of the Pennines, in the valley of the River Wenning. The great bulk of Ingleborough lies five miles to the north east, the ancient City of Lancaster is fifteen miles to the west, Settle is to the east and Westmorland a few miles to the north.

The Grammar School was established in 1726 and, following a re-organisation in 1877, it supplied secondary education for about forty boys on a fee-paying basis. The teaching staff consisted of the headmaster and one assistant master. The wife of the headmaster was expected to take an interest in the boarders and a full part in the running of the school. The headmaster's salary was £120 a year, as it had been since 1876, although accommodation was provided for him and his family. Most of the pupils were the sons of farmers and tradespeople.

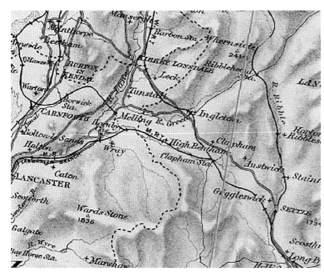

Map of Bentham area.

In 1907, the previous headmaster decided to retire. There was a large field of 101 applicants for the post. Theodore Hardy was appointed. It may have helped that he had taught the son of the retiring headmaster at Nottingham High School. Apart from the obvious attraction of becoming master of his own school, there were other factors in his wish to obtain the post. He loved the countryside and the opportunities it gave for fell walking and cycling. Bentham was conveniently placed for the boat from Heysham to Northern Ireland, bringing contact with Florence's family much closer. Bentham had its own railway station connecting to the West Coast main line. By this time Elizabeth was ready to begin her degree at London University and trains to London could be caught with a change at Lancaster. William was given a scholarship at Rossall School, not too far away in Fleetwood. Theodore was also welcomed by the local clergy who could use him as a *locum tenens*.

Bentham was a straggling community with a population of just under 2,500. Effectively it was formed of two settlements, High Bentham and Low Bentham, together with farmsteads in the surrounding countryside. In addition to the Anglican Church there was a strong Methodist presence, but there was also a powerful Quaker influence in the area. The Ford family were prominent Quakers and employers who owned the local silk mill. Research by Cyril Pearce of Leeds University has shown that during the war there were 31 conscientious objectors from Bentham – an unusually high number as a proportion to the 209 who served in the forces.

Hardy threw himself into his new job, and was soon appreciated. 'Mr Hardy won the admiration of all pupils, parents and friends by his whole-hearted enthusiasm in his work, his charming manly virtues, his purity and simplicity of character.'[1]

The official *History of Bentham Grammar School* states that Hardy 'believed in hard work and hard play and set the standard himself. He was first to take the plunge into the river when a new swimming club was launched. He stressed the health of the locality in the School Prospectus, and set up a gymnasium in the school. He underpinned the emphasis on healthy living with his own example of being teetotal and a vegetarian.'

His habit of travelling everywhere by bicycle sometimes ended in hilarity as far as the pupils were concerned. Poor eyesight meant that he kept falling off his bike, and he would frequently appear at breakfast with a black eye after running into a gate. Yet the hilarity was based on genuine affection for the man.

The school offered a broad curriculum, going beyond the traditional academic subjects. Hardy's predecessor, John Llewellyn, had wisely introduced an element of science with an agricultural slant and book-keeping. Hardy's love of music added a further dimension to the school.

Theodore Hardy was to stay at Bentham for six years.

His arrival at Bentham coincided with a direction from the Board of Education in the Campbell-Bannerman Liberal Government requiring all maintained secondary schools to reserve a percentage of their entry for pupils from elementary schools. It was an attempt to widen secondary education and involved the award of 'scholarships' by which the local authority would pay tuition fees. It had a negative impact on Bentham Grammar School which was independent and it limited numbers for a few years, when some local boys went to either Giggleswick or Lancaster Grammar School on county scholarships.

Under Hardy's prompting the governors altered their 1877 scheme in order to make Anglican instruction available, rather than obligatory, and to extend the curriculum along the same lines as the maintained secondary

The Reverend T.B. Hardy, Headmaster, and boys of Bentham Grammar School, circa 1908.

The Headmaster's house, Bentham Grammar School.

The School-room, Bentham Grammar School, as Hardy would have known it. This was the only classroom in Hardy's time. The photograph was taken in the 1920s, by which time it had become known as 'Hardy Hall' in remembrance of the former headmaster.

schools. This ensured that Bentham received grants from both the Board of Education and West Riding County Council. Again under Hardy's prompting it was decided to award eight scholarships to local boys if their parents agreed to continue secondary education for at least two years.[2]

All was going well. The Hardy family was liked and respected by both the school and the village. The boarders had a special affection for the lively and amusing Mrs Hardy, when disaster struck... Florence was found to be seriously ill with cancer and given only a short time to live in the summer of 1913.

It was a devastating blow for the whole family. They were a close and unusually loving family. William was by now reading medicine at Queens University in Belfast, whilst Elizabeth was at London University. Both desperately wanted to be at home with their mother, and a letter from Theodore to William at this time talks of a tearful farewell on the Bentham Road.

It was clearly impossible for Florence to carry on her work at the school and Theodore felt the need to be with her and to nurse her through her illness. He submitted his resignation to the governors, and it was arranged through the Vicar of Kirkby Lonsdale and the Bishop of Carlisle that he should take over the living of the parish of Hutton Roof as priest-in-charge.[3]

Hutton Roof was, and is, a scattered rural community near Kirkby Lonsdale at the southern end of Westmorland (now Cumbria). It is an area of rolling hills and narrow country lanes. Most of the land belonged to the Lowther family. The small squat church nestles under the shadow of the limestone Hutton Roof Crags. Bentham is ten miles away to the south-west across the River Lune. Ingleborough Hill still dominates the landscape. The people have a slow, regular way of life, a way of life usually marked with courtesy and consideration for others. In Hardy's time it had a population, with Lupton, of about 600. Here the Hardys were made welcome by their new parishioners.

Hutton Roof was mostly rural, but it still had a mixture of miners and slate workers in the quarries. Hardy's stipend was £169 per year and the family was provided with a comfortable late Victorian vicarage. He was responsible for the care of two churches, St John the Divine in Hutton Roof and All Saints Church Lupton, which was two miles away along a narrow twisting country lane. Both settlements had small schools close by the church.

The Hardy family in September 1905. The photograph was taken at Thurlby Vicarage, Lincolnshire.

Theodore Hardy's cousin, Miss Bessie Hardy, came up from Devon to help them settle in and has left a graphic description of their new home: 'The scenery all the way was magnificent – we turned up a little lane some distance from the main entrance to the vicarage, just at the foot of the Crag, crossed a hayfield, and then through a little wicket, at the end of a terrace and avenue of firs, beeches, sycamores and chestnuts; rose-beds were dotted along a grass walk just below the terrace; great moss-grown boulders jutted out at intervals, and halfway along the terrace were an old archway and mossy steps leading down to the rose-beds; a few yards further and we came to the conservatory, through which we entered the south side of the vicarage into the dining-room. Looking through the front window the view was indeed a transformation – now we were gazing on the majestic grandeur of Ingleborough.'[4]

But despite the beauty it was a house of sadness. In June 1914, on a Sunday morning, Theodore went across to the church to pray. When he returned, William told him that Florence had died. After Theodore performed the Funeral Service she was buried near to the entrance gate to the churchyard.

In the same month, a shot rang out in Sarajevo which was to change the history of the world. Within five short weeks of the assassination of the Archduke of Austria, events moved on to lead to a World War which would change, and end, the lives of millions.

In Hutton Roof, life had to carry on. Hardy's answer to his sorrow was predictable; he threw himself into his work. He would also go for long walks on the Crag by himself and in a letter to Mary Hardy he told of how he had 'met consolation, even refreshment on the way'.[5] His faith had survived the test.

In October, cousin Bessie returned again permanently to be the housekeeper when Elizabeth went back to university. She again gives a vivid description of life at Hutton Roof Vicarage: 'The vicarage was literally open house; very seldom were the doors locked; all visitors were hospitably welcomed – tramps were given a good meal and a hot pot of tea; on one occasion I remember going for a conveyance so that a poor woman could be driven to the nearest workhouse, where she was trying to walk under great difficulties, her feet being badly ulcerated; after rest and a good dinner, she and her husband were driven off, amidst grateful thanks to his "Riverence".'

Bessie went on to describe how Theodore adopted a gun-shy dog which would otherwise have been put down. On one occasion a monster rat escaped from the cat into the drawing room. Hardy opened the window and said, 'Let it get free, it has fought for its life'.[6]

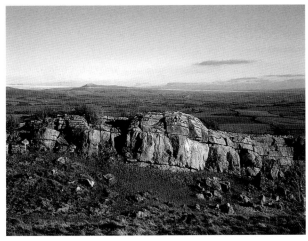

Hutton Roof Craggs, Ingleborough in the distance.

Hutton Roof Vicarage.

It was at this time that Hardy met a young man who was to develop into a larger than life, well known country character in Kirkby Lonsdale, the town blacksmith, Jonty Wilson. Jonty was to become the subject of a biography by Dalesman publications. Jonty became the assistant scoutmaster.

It became the custom in later years for Jonty to give the valediction, 'We will remember them', in Kirkby Lonsdale parish church on Remembrance Sunday.

He often recalled Theodore Hardy in his address to the congregation. 'As a young man I acted as Assistant Scoutmaster to the 1st Kirkby Lonsdale Troop of Boy Scouts. We had a permanent camp on Hutton Roof Crags and during the summer months spent many happy weekends there. That is how I first met Mr Hardy and a friendship developed which lasted until his death in Rouen in 1918. Often on weekday nights I would go to Hutton Roof and call at the vicarage for Mr Hardy. We would creep up the crag in the dusk to spend nights in the camp. Lovely

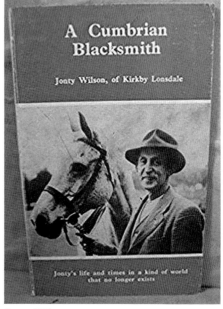

Jonty Wilson.

Hutton Roof Vicarage,
Kirkby Lonsdale.
27 - viii - 15.

Dear Corporal Wilson,

Having heard from your father that you have been some time at the Front, I am writing to congratulate you on taking part in the splendid work that is being done by our army abroad. I hope that you may come back safe and sound

but still more that you may be ... to keep up to the very high standard of duty set by your Comrades. I know that you have things to face which most of us could hardly have imagined, ... but if you ... going at them in the spirit in which you went at your scout work, I am sure you will be able to answer as a British soldier should any call that is made on you. You won't forget, I think, from whom the

strength comes. — I could enter well into your father's feelings of pride and anxiety, because my son is at the Front too: he is in the R.A.M.C. and is at present very near the Dardanelles, working in a "Stationary" hospital and field ambulances.

I should like very much, a short letter telling me something about your experiences, as far as the censor will allow; — but I don't want you to bother to write if you are busy ...

if — like a good many people — you dislike letter-writing: — just send me a post-card to say you have had this and — I hope — a little joy parcel I am getting Theobien to send.

... wishing you God speed,

I am, Yours sincerely,
T.W.Hardy.

Hardy Letter.

scented nights they were, with the smell of bracken and juniper, the steep hillsides dotted with glow worms and the nightjar "jerring" from the rocky out-crops on the tops'.[7]

When war came in 1914, Jonty joined as a volunteer with the Westmorland and Cumberland Yeomanry. A correspondence continued between them until Hardy's death. One of those letters to Jonty in August 1915 is reproduced in this book. It indicates Hardy's attitude to the war, and also his wish to know what is going on. The letter still has the black band of mourning over twelve months after Florence's death.

When Jonty heard that Hardy had been wounded he was given permission to visit him, but on arrival at the hospital he was told by a nurse (also from Hutton Roof) that it was too late. Jonty was the only non-commissioned officer to attend Theodore Hardy's funeral in Rouen.

Two other letters written by Hardy at that time survive. Both were to William, who graduated and qualified as a doctor in March 1915. The letters reveal Hardy's feelings about his wife's death, his warmth, love and admiration for his children, his generosity despite a lack of wealth, and a willingness (despite his poor sight) to undertake a fifteen mile cycle ride in the middle of the night before a Sunday service.

Hutton Roof Vicarage
23 March 1915

Dear Will,

I can't go to bed without writing my congratulations although I hope you have started for home before this letter reaches Belfast. It is splendid to think that you have really done it and we are sure that Mother knows this and is glad with us – to whom, under God, you chiefly owe it. I must say also that I am very, very proud of you, Will, for I know how real the difficulties you have had and the temptations to steer clear of. I don't think you will ever forget those Goodbyes in the road at Bentham. As to difficulties, on the score of health alone no one could have blamed you at all if you had taken at least a year longer, and many would have taken more than that.

Well, now you have got the degree, thank God for that, a real step in life, up to a position of power for good, and I pray God that you always use it with a sense of your responsibility to Him. I am sure that Mother is praying with me that your life as a man may be worthy, and in thanking Him for the past. I hope you have sent a telegram to Elizabeth, but I shall send one tomorrow when I send yours – to make sure.

With much love and heartiest congratulations.
From your affectionate and proud
Father.

Twenty-four hours later he wrote another letter – in a much lighter vein. He had decided to go to Belfast for the graduation ceremony.

Hutton Roof
24.3.15

Dear Doctor,

   I am sorry I cannot reply to your letter, which came by the morning post, sooner than by tomorrow morning, but I suppose it isn't necessary to telegraph. I have made out with some searching of timetables that I can get over for Saturday, and shall be very glad indeed to come. I didn't think the presentation for degrees would be so soon. Please thank Aunt Mary for asking me to stay, but I shall come by the Saturday morning Heysham boat and go back by Stranraer: you know I like railway travelling and I hope to get a good sleep on the train and in the Heysham boat if the weather is good. I can get back to Carnforth by 1.30 am Sunday and shall leave my bicycle there going. Will you come back with me or have you made other plans? I should be very glad if you did, but it seems a pity to hurry away, if there is anything you would like to do, and I shouldn't see much of you on Sunday.

   Elsie Peck is staying over Sunday but it isn't sure whether Elizabeth will be able to come or not, because of a lecture that may be given.

   I have written this cheque for £12 – Mind this is all my business, it is only once in my lifetime I have a son's medical degrees to pay for and I enjoy it – This leaves me a fair balance [the words 'This doesn't overdraw by a good deal' are crossed out] and I have an instalment of £20 odd, I think, coming on April 5th. I went into Mathews, after sending my telegram to you this morning. They were very nice and interested and complimentary to you. I won't write more now as I hope I shall be seeing you soon.

With love and congratulations (once more),
Your affectionate Father.[8]

Theodore's cheque is equivalent to over a thousand pounds today.

Shortly after graduating William volunteered to join the Royal Army Medical Corps on 15 May 1915. Within days he sailed for Egypt to care for casualties from the ill-fated Dardanelles campaign. He was based in Ismailia on the Suez Canal but often travelled to the Dardanelles on hospital ships to help bring out the wounded. At first his rank was lieutenant, quickly made up to captain, and then in 1916, up to major.

His sister Elizabeth, having completed her studies at London University, had also volunteered as a nurse in the Red Cross. She was based in Dunkirk where, three years later, she had a joyful reunion with her father.

Theodore too, even at the age of 51, felt that he should be involved in the war. Time after time he applied to the Chaplaincy Department, only to be

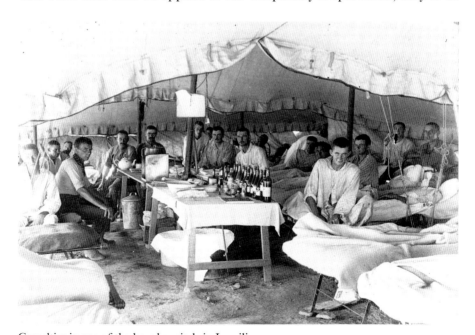

Casualties in one of the base hospitals in Ismailia.

told that they had a long waiting list of men much younger than himself. He seriously thought of going not as a chaplain, but as a volunteer stretcher bearer. He attended an ambulance class in Kirkby Lonsdale and successfully passed the first aid examination. Hardy was not a man to be deflected, and his persistence finally paid off. He was called for interview in the summer of 1916, and to his great delight was accepted. The Battle of the Somme had not only produced a shortage of troops, it had produced a shortage of chaplains. It may have been that his old friend from Nottingham days, Llewellyn Gwynne, by now a bishop and Assistant Chaplain General with overall command of all chaplains on the Western Front, had intervened on his behalf. His rank was to be that of a captain. His actual title, given future events, has a hint of irony. He was to be a temporary chaplain, 4th class.

Chapter Five

To be a Padre

'There's no discouragement, shall make him once relent…'

By the end of August 1916, the new temporary chaplain 4th class was fully kitted out, given a captain's uniform with the distinctive Maltese Cross badge, and a travel warrant from Charing Cross via Folkestone and Boulogne to France. His destination was the huge base camp of Étaples, set amongst the sand dunes on the Channel coast.

Étaples must have been a bewildering contrast to the peace and tranquillity of Hutton Roof in rural Westmorland. At its height, well over one hundred thousand men were accommodated and put through intensive training for the front. Bugles would ring out for reveille at 5.30 am summer and winter alike, and the base would resound to the shouts and yells of the 'canary' instructors in the dreaded Bull Ring training ground set amongst the sand dunes. It was a desolate and hated place. It was the scene of a major mutiny in September 1917, which threatened to bring the Passchendaele offensive to a halt.[1]

The poet Wilfred Owen described Étaples in a letter home: 'I lay awake in a windy tent in the middle of a vast, dreadful encampment. It seemed neither France nor England, but a kind of paddock where the beasts are kept a few days before the shambles. I heard the revelling of the Scotch troops, who are now dead, and who knew they would be dead. I thought of the very strange look on all faces in that camp; an incomprehensible look, which a man will never see in England; nor can it be seen in any battle. But only in Étaples. It was not despair, or terror, it was more terrible than terror, for it was a blindfold look, and without expression, like a dead rabbit's.'[2]

The 'Bull Ring', Étaples.

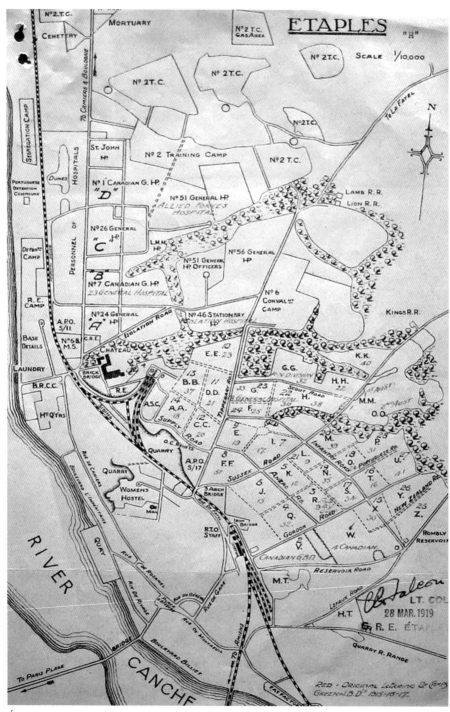

Étaples base.

When Theodore Hardy arrived the base was humming with activity. New units were being trained and sent to take part in the second month of the great offensive on the Somme. Over a hundred trains a day took reinforcements up to the line and brought back the dying and the wounded. Between 1 July and 16 November 1916, British losses on the Somme totalled nearly 420,000. He was posted to two Infantry Base Depots in the Reinforcement Area of Étaples. There was a continual turnover of men, and it was virtually impossible to make more than the merest contact with any individual before they were gone.

The base at Étaples was situated on the sand dunes next to the Channel, south of Boulogne at the mouth of the River Canche. It was the largest British base in France. Hardy spent four months there in the autumn of 1916. Here, he had to come to terms his role as an army chaplain. Having at long last won the battle to gain admission into the Chaplaincy, he showed the same persistence in pressing for what he really wanted, a posting to the front line.

His old friend Llewellyn Gwynne, and former Vicar of St Andrews, Nottingham, was by now Deputy Chaplain General in France. It is possible that Bishop Gwynne recommended Hardy and helped him to overcome the difficulty of being accepted as an over age padre in 1916. The Assistant Chaplain General, the Reverend Douglas Carey, was to write of Hardy's interview, 'Normally one hesitated to recommend a Chaplain of over 50 years of age [Hardy was almost 54] for work in the line, but I have been intensely glad ever since that I had the common sense to see that it was with no ordinary mortal that I had to deal on this occasion. He had done good work during his time with me; he told me that he had always kept fit, had done regular physical exercises, and had been accustomed to a cold bath daily all the year round. He also stated that he was a widower, that both his children were grown up, and that he had no fear of death. His appeal was irresistible. I recommended his case to the Deputy Chaplain General, and, to his joy, my recommendation was acted upon.'[3]

Hardy knew with instinctive certainty that the front line was the place where he ought to be. When he got there he was to demonstrate by action as much as by words what that certainty meant. Knowing what to do, and getting on with it, marked him out as different from a great many other chaplains who, though well intentioned, came in for severe criticism both during and after the war.

Alan Lloyd in his book *The War in the Trenches* notes that 'first-hand accounts of trench warfare suggest a conspicuous absence of padres in the forward lines – a curious omission when, as Bishop W.C. Wand (himself a chaplain) noted later, the war was making even the most careless face the issues of life and death; and when the fundamental questions of religion and philosophy had to be tackled afresh.'[4]

Siegfried Sassoon, after he was wounded near Arras wrote, 'The Dressing Station was a small underground place crowded with groaning wounded. Two doctors were doing what they could for men who had paid a heavy price for their freedom. My egocentricity diminished among all that agony. I remember listening to an emotional padre who was painfully aware that he could do nothing except stand about and feel sympathetic. The consolations of the Church of England weren't much in demand at an Advance Dressing Station.'[5] One must feel some sympathy for the misery and sadness of that inadequate cleric. Yet as we will see, standing around with wringing hands was not what Theodore Hardy became known for.

Perhaps the most devastating criticism of the chaplains came from Hardy's old school friend C.E. Montague. In the chapter 'The Sheep that Were Not Fed' in his book *Disenchantment*, written soon after the war, Montague writes, 'There were all sorts and conditions of men among them [the chaplains], some good; some bad, like the chaplain drunk at dinner in Gobert's restaurant in Amiens on the evening of one of the bloodiest days of the first battle of the Somme. There was the man, who urged by national comradeship, would have been a soldier but that his bishop banned it: to be an army chaplain was the next best thing. There was the man who, urged by a different instinct, felt irresistibly that at that moment the war was the central thing in the whole world and that it was unbearable not to be at the centre of things. And there was, in great force, the large, healthy, pleasant young curate … He abounded so much that whenever now one hears the words "Army Chaplain" his large genial image springs up of itself in the mind.' Montague went on to conclude that, consciously or unconsciously, men at the front acquired a receptiveness to spiritual values which presented the churches with a unique opportunity. Yet, 'Nobody used it: the tide in the affairs of churches flowed its best, but no church came to take it. Instead, as if chance had planned a kind of satiric practical epigram, came the brigade chaplain. As soon as his genial bulk hove in sight, and his cheery rumbustious chaff began blowing about, the shy and uncouth muse of our savage theology unfolded her wings and flew away. Once more the talk was all footer and rations and scragging the Kaiser.'[6]

There could also be a tragic sectarian narrowness which brought heart-breaking grief. A devout Scottish soldier serving in an English regiment wrote home from the front to say that he was about to take part in an attack, but that he had been refused communion by the Anglican padre. The soldier was killed in the attack.[7]

Yet it is too easy and simplistic to criticise men finding themselves facing a situation so profoundly and horrifically different to the often small world of the pre-war Church. One must remember, too, that social differences were sharp and there was bound to be a communication gap between a largely middle class clergy and the other ranks of the British Army. It is not surprising that many were found wanting.

A pre-war survey of the City of York showed that only twenty-eight per cent of the population were church goers, and that of this group the vast majority were middle class with women outnumbering men.[8]

Robert Graves asserted that, 'Hardly one soldier in a hundred was inspired by religious feeling of even the crudest kind.' Whilst this may be an overstatement, John Baynes, an officer who made a study of morale on the Western Front, reckoned that one ranker in every two attached no importance to religion in the trenches, and yet, 'Many would laugh at religion one day and pray most sincerely the next, particularly if under heavy shell fire. My estimate is that forty per cent reacted in this way.'[9]

Bernard Martin, a lieutenant in the 64th Foot, remembered being given his identity discs, which, despite the fact that he was a member of the Church of Scotland, had 'C. of E.' stamped on them:

'Why do you put a chap's religion on the disc, sergeant?'

He laughed. 'Precaution, sir, precaution. In war you never can tell.'

'Tell what?'

'Why, sir, if your number should happen to come up, you wouldn't want the chaplains to quarrel about who's to bury you.'

'I'm not really C. of E.,' I observed mildly.

The sergeant said in the tone of a wise man talking to an inexperienced youth, 'You stick to C. of E., sir. You wouldn't want to be buried by the Pope, I'm sure.'

I laughed. 'I don't suppose it makes any difference.'

'Oh, it does make a difference, sir.' He spoke earnestly. 'It does. RCs go to Hell before they get to Heaven – that's official. RCs call it Purgatory. You're definitely better off as C. of E., sir.'

Martin again describes the climate of religious feeling when writing of a church parade. 'I don't know who ordered the church parades when we came out on Rest. During my first eight months we had ten, but only three in seven months of 1917. I liked these parades, they were simple, no rituals or theology, only hymns, a lesson read from the Bible and a short address by the chaplain. (In the front line we had no religion – that is no church parades, no regular visits from our chaplain.) The men were indifferent though most sang the hymns, probably to words other than those printed in the hymn books.'[10]

This was the challenge of horror, indifference and inadequacy that Theodore Hardy had to face when he was told that he was to join the 8th Battalion of the Lincolnshire Regiment and the 8th Battalion of the Somerset Light Infantry in early December 1916. Douglas Carey, the Assistant Chaplain General, responded to a request for some tips by introducing him to a fellow chaplain just down from the line. It was to be a meeting of two of the most extraordinary men to have served in the war, who between them more than redeemed for the mistakes and inadequacies of others. Early in December 1916, Theodore Hardy spent an hour meeting Geoffrey Studdert Kennedy in Douglas Carey's office in Étaples.

Both men were to get beyond the outward show of formal religion to penetrate a deeper communion of souls; the sense of brotherhood and comradeship which produced a bond between soldier and soldier, a true communion where men shouldered the burdens of their weaker mates, risked their lives to rescue a comrade, and would try to help the families of dead friends. Both men knew that to penetrate this brotherhood they had to be part of it.

Chapter Six

A Meeting with Woodbine Willie

It isn't proved, you fool, it can't be proved.
How can you prove a victory before
It's won? How can you prove a man who leads
To be a leader worth the following,
Unless you follow to the death?

Faith – Geoffrey Studdert Kennedy

Theodore Hardy and Geoffrey Studdert Kennedy make a remarkable contrast, yet they warmed to one another immediately. Studdert Kennedy was twenty years younger than Hardy, and had been a chaplain for just over a year. He came from an Anglo-Irish family although he was brought up in Leeds where his father was the Rector of St Mary's in Quarry Hill. It was a deeply impoverished area of squalid back-to-backs, one-room cottages, cramped yards and courts with foul open drains and shared middens. Outbreaks of cholera were particularly bad. Smoky mills and a vast foundry polluted the air. Geoffrey grew up helping with his father's parish work, getting to know the people. The experience gave him a profound affection for the poor, a deep admiration for their spirit and courage, and a fierce hatred of social injustice.

When he met Theodore Hardy he was becoming well known, and was on

The Reverend Geoffrey Anketell Studdert Kennedy MC (27 June 1883–8 March 1929).

the brink of the enormous fame which was to follow and bestow upon him the name of 'Woodbine Willie'.

He combined the clownish pathos of Chaplin with the nervous eloquence and wit of Nye Bevan and the radical Irish forthrightness of Bob Geldof. His biographer describes the large bat-wing ears; the mouth giving an impression of being over large for its surroundings; but the most remarkable feature of his physical appearance was his eyes. 'They were very large, very brown; but also for some reason or other – quite extraordinarily sad. Many people have sad eyes in this world, and with reason. But here it seems were eyes reflecting deep within themselves a sadness more profound, more elemental than anything arising from the mere slings and arrows of outrageous fortune. Here were eyes, in fact, whose sadness seemed to be of another worldly dimension, as though the possessor of them had found God himself in tears.'[1]

He suffered dreadfully from asthma. Despite this he rescued the wounded during gas attacks on the Messines Ridge in June 1917 and was awarded the Military Cross. Like Hardy, he was later appointed to be a chaplain to the King.

At Étaples, despite the prevailing indifference to things religious, he could pack a hall with tough Australians wanting to hear him speak. He could startle an audience into attention with the words, 'I know what you're thinking, here comes the bloody parson.' He masked the Celtic sadness with an outrageously amusing wit and humour. He wrote poetry of immense power in a Kiplingesque style and meter.

When he arrived in France, he told Assistant Chaplain General Douglas Carey that at one time he had been 'a revolutionary agnostic socialist who used to stand on a tub and talk in public places in the Midlands'. His reward for disclosing this piece of information was to be sent to minister to the needs of the troops passing through the canteen of Rouen railway station on their way to the front. Here he would 'stand on a box and announce to the crowds of soldiery that he was about to sing *Mother Machree* for the sons, *Little Grey Home in the West* for the husbands, *The Sunshine of your Smile* for the lovers. Afterwards he would offer to write home for them, and was seen to be doing so, surrounded by a throng pressing in on him. And when the time came for them to go, he would be by the train as it pulled out until he was left, heavy with his thoughts, to watch its vanishing tail-light.'[2]

Studdert Kennedy, who could reach the hearts and minds of so many otherwise indifferent, could also be grossly misunderstood, as when General Plumer, all red cheeks and white moustache, stormed out of a sermon and demanded his removal from the chaplaincy.

Yet the great meetings, clowning boxing matches with the champion Jimmy Driscoll, all of these things and more, took second place to where Studdert Kennedy wanted to be – at the front. He had just returned from the Gommecourt section after the Somme offensive when he met Hardy, and it was of the front that they talked.

In a post-war letter to Mary Hardy, Studdert Kennedy wrote of their meeting. He gives a vivid picture of Hardy (and, incidentally, of himself). 'I remember the conversation very well, and the memory has never left me. I would not have dared to hope that it could really have exercised an influence on Hardy's glorious life, and your letter makes me feel very glad and very small. I will describe the interview as I remember it. I had come down from the line, to my great disappointment, having been recalled to preach the National Mission. I was sick as mud at being recalled, and full of longing to get back to work in the line about which I was enthusiastic. Mr Carey told me of a wonderful man who was serving with him, and had specially applied to go up the line, although he really was too old. He said Mr Hardy would like very much to talk with me before he went up, and get some "tips" about the work, and had asked him to arrange an interview. I was very glad to do what I could.

'He came to me at Mr Carey's office. I remember what struck me first was that he was not young and not strong. Then as I talked I began to feel quite honestly that this man was a kind of saint. I think it was his humility, and utter willingness to learn, and his eagerness for sacrifice that struck me – most of all his humility.

'He asked me to tell him what the best way of working up there was. I said, "Live with the men. Go everywhere they go. Make up your mind that you will share all their risks, and more if you can do any good. You can take it that the best place for a Padre (provided he does not interfere with military operations) is where there is most danger of death. Our first job is to go beyond the men in self-sacrifice and reckless devotion. Don't be bamboozled into believing that your proper place is behind the line; it isn't. If you stay behind you might as well come down, you won't do a ha'porth of good. Your place is in the front. The line is the key to the whole business. Work in the front, and they will listen to you when they come out to rest, but if you only preach and teach behind, you are wasting time, the men won't pay the slightest attention to you. The men will forgive you anything but lack of courage and devotion; without that you are useless." I remember walking up and down and saying this very fiercely, because I was full of it. He took it all so humbly and eagerly that I was ashamed of myself, and loved him. Then I said, "The Devil tries to get at you by telling you that you could really do no good in the line, and that you were more use alive than dead. It was the Devil and a lie – the more Padres died in battle doing Christ-like deeds, the better for the Church. Most of us will be more use dead than alive!"

'I remember we both looked at one another when I blundered out with that odd speech, and laughed. Then he asked me about purely spiritual work and the opportunities for it.

'I said, "There is very little purely spiritual work, it is all muddled and mixed – but it is all spiritual. Take a box of fags in your haversack and a great deal of love in your heart, and go up to them, laugh with them, joke with them; you can pray with them sometimes, but pray for them always."

'As we talked he got more enthusiastic. The programme appealed to him, and I loved him because it appealed, and I felt that he would do it all much better than I had ever been able to do, because he had the power that belongs to saints, and I was just such a beastly ordinary man.

'I told him some yarns, and we both roared, laughing over them. Then I was interrupted and had to go to a meeting. We shook hands, and I have never seen him since, but I loved him then, and I love him now. He is one of the best, and God must enjoy him tremendously. If I did influence him, it is just another proof of the queer instruments God can use to do jobs with, but I believe that, if he had never seen me or heard of me, he would inevitably have done what he did, because he was in his soul a hero and a saint.

'P.S. – On reading this I find that Hardy says nothing – that was what he really did say; he just didn't speak much; he listened and was himself, and he looked pure, fine enthusiasm.'[3]

Although they never met again, there is no doubt Geoffrey Studdert Kennedy did indeed make a profound impression on Theodore Hardy. Hardy himself was to say as much when he answered a letter of congratulations from Douglas Carey upon the award of his VC eighteen months later: 'Are

Studdert Kennedy.

you likely to meet or write to Studdert Kennedy soon? If so, will you tell him that I have often wished I could thank him properly for that hour in your office which, more than almost any other in my life, has helped me in this work – you must admit that you can understand how I feel about these ribbons when I think of him!'[4]

A few days before Hardy went to join his new battalion, Douglas Carey saw him at the Chaplains' School in St Omer. He was, noted Carey, supremely happy. To a member of his family, Hardy said at this time that all his previous life and work had been but a preparation, a leading up to his work as a Chaplain; all his life it would seem, he had been haunted by a sort of dream of some curious and great experience that was waiting for him.[5]

> '*…and Evangelist gave him one smile, and bid him God-Speed, so he went on with haste.*'
>
> *Pilgrim's Progress*, John Bunyan

HIS MATE

> There's a broken, battered village,
> Somewhere up behind the line,
> There's a dug-out and a bunk there
> That I used to say were mine.
>
> I remember how I reached them,
> Dripping wet and all forlorn,

In the dim and dreary twilight
Of a weeping summer morn.

All that week I'd buried brothers,
In one bitter battle slain,
In one grave I laid two hundred.
God! What sorrow and what rain!

And that night I'd been in trenches,
Seeking out the sodden dead,
And just dropping them in shell-holes,
With a service swiftly said.

For the bullets rattled round me,
But I couldn't leave them there,
Water-soaked in flooded shell-holes,
Reft of common Christian prayer.

So I crawled round on my belly,
And I listened to the roar
Of the guns that hammered Thiepval,
Like big breakers on the shore.

Then there spoke a dripping sergeant,
When the time was growing late,
'Would you please to bury this one,
'Cause 'e used to be my mate?'

So we groped our way in darkness
To a body lying there,
Just a blacker lump of blackness,
With a red blotch on his hair.

Though we turned him gently over,
Yet I still can hear the thud,
As the body fell face forward,
And then settled in the mud.

We went down upon our faces,
And I said the service through,
From 'I am the Resurrection'
To the last, the great 'adieu'.

We stood up to give the Blessing,
And commend him to the Lord,
When a sudden light shot soaring
Silver swift and like a sword.

At a stroke it slew the darkness,
Flashed its glory on the mud,
And I saw the sergeant staring
At a crimson clot of blood.
There are many kinds of sorrow
In this world of Love and Hate,
But there is no sterner sorrow
Than a soldier's for his mate.

Geoffrey Studdert Kennedy

"I know thy works : behold, I have set before thee an open door, and no man can shut it : for thou hast a little strength, and has kept my word, and hast not denied my name". Revelations 3.8

Chapter Seven

To the Front Line

'He chose the Cross: that was his way henceforth. Now there's a glamour even about the Cross until you actually shoulder it, and then if there is any glamour at all, it is only other people who see it.'

Mary Hardy, T.B. Hardy's sister-in-law, 1919[1]

When Theodore Hardy arrived in France in August 1916, the British sector of the front ran from the Channel coast in Belgium to south of Albert in Picardy, in the department of the Somme. In December his wish to be at the Front was granted. He travelled by train from Étaples to the railhead at Doullens. He then went by foot for six miles, with 160 reinforcements, to Sarton, a small commune in the Pas-de-Calais in the northern back-area of the Somme. Here, with the reinforcements, he joined the 8th (Service) Battalion of the Lincolnshire Regiment. Appropriately, given Mary Hardy's comments at the head of this chapter, the road out of the village towards the front line was dominated by an enormous cast iron crucifix.

Within days, the Lincolns were joined again by the 8th (S) Battalion Somerset Light Infantry returning from the Gommecourt sector trenches of the Somme. Hardy now had responsibility for the care of up to 2,000 men if the two battalions ever returned to full strength. Hardy was fortunate to have Lieutenant Colonel John Willoughby Scott as the Somerset's commanding officer and Lieutenant John Hay Maitland Hardyman as their adjutant. Both were highly intelligent and unusual men; Hardy enjoyed their company and their support and grew close to them both.

John Willoughby Scott was 38 and extremely well connected. He was also a very brave officer awarded the DSO and mentioned in despatches three times. He was educated at Rugby and in peacetime was a barrister. His father, Sir John Scott, was the Deputy Judge Advocate General during the second Boer War, and his mother was a niece of Sir Rowland Hill of Post

The Western Front, mid–1916, before the Somme.[2]

3. - SARTON (P.-de-C.). - Eglise et Mairie

Charles Ueidej, Arras

Collection-jfm.fr

The ancient church in Sarton with the *mairie* on the right.

Lieutenant Colonel John Willoughby Scott DSO, 8th (Service) Battalion, Somerset Light Infantry.

Lieutenant J.H. Maitland Hardyman DSO MC, 8th (Service) Battalion, Somerset Light Infantry.

Office fame. His brother was also a barrister, Conservative MP for Liverpool Exchange, Solicitor General in the Lloyd George coalition government and eventually a high court judge.

Lieutenant Colonel Scott had served in the second Boer War in the Queen's Oxfordshire Hussars – a rather smart cavalry yeomanry regiment where his friends included Jack Spencer-Churchill and his brother Winston. In 1914 the Oxfordshire Hussars had been mobilised and attached as personal bodyguard to Sir John French, Commander-in-Chief of the British Expeditionary Force. Guarding Sir John in St Omer soon paled and John Scott's request to go to the front resulted in his appointment to command the 8th Somersets.

Second Lieutenant John Hay Maitland Hardyman became the adjutant of the 8th Somerset's shortly before Hardy joined the battalion. He was 22. He was a remarkable young man and went on to command the battalion at the age of 23, becoming the youngest ever lieutenant colonel in the British Army. He served with Hardy for almost the entire period of Hardy's time at the front. It is fair to say he appreciated Theodore Hardy, and Hardy appreciated him. Sadly, Hardyman was killed on 24 August 1918, just a few weeks before Hardy. His parents inscribed, 'Scholar, Poet, Orator Justified by Faith in Jesus Christ' on his headstone. It is a huge loss today not to have a record of their conversations, for talk they did, and it would be fascinating to know of what they talked.

Maitland Hardyman, the son of a Scottish surgeon, was born in Bath. He was educated in Edinburgh with an open scholarship at Fettes and admitted to Edinburgh University at the age of 17. He was a brilliant student, winning academic prizes in the Arts faculty and was on the Student Representative Council in 1912, 1913 and 1914. Student politics brought him into contact with Ramsay MacDonald and he was active in the fledgling Labour Party. On graduation in 1914 he became principal assistant to the Director of Edinburgh Zoo, but within days of the outbreak of war he joined the Somerset Light Infantry as a private.

After a brief spell with the Royal Flying Corps he was commissioned in the Somerset Light Infantry in January 1915. After serving on the brigade and divisional staffs he was appointed adjutant of the 8th Somerset Light Infantry. He was wounded on the Somme in November 1916, shortly before Hardy arrived.

Despite the fact that Maitland Hardyman fought in the war, he was also a member of the National Council of the Union of Democratic Control (UDC). The UDC was founded by a group of radical Liberal and Labour MPs who objected to the way in which Britain had been drawn into the war. The founders included E.D. Morel, Charles Trevelyan MP, Arthur Ponsonby MP, Ramsay MacDonald MP, and Bertrand Russell.

They believed the main reason for the conflict was secret diplomacy, including that conducted by Sir Edward Grey, the British Foreign Secretary. They had three main objectives:

1. In future to prevent secret diplomacy there should be parliamentary control over foreign policy.
2. There should be negotiations after the war with other democratic European countries in an attempt to form an organisation to help prevent future conflicts.
3. That at the end of the war the peace terms should neither humiliate the defeated nation nor artificially rearrange frontiers, as this might provide a cause for future wars.[3]

The UDC did not call for an immediate end to the war, but for a full examination of war aims in public and by Parliament. It strongly opposed conscription and wartime censorship along with other restrictions on civil liberties. It was largely financed by donations from Quakers and Charles Trevelyan. It was denounced by the right wing press as unpatriotic and they paid for its meetings to be broken up.

Hardyman took a risk by keeping in touch with the leadership and attending UDC meetings when he was on leave. 'He was in constant correspondence with those at home whom it was most dangerous for him, from a military point of view, even to agree with.'[4]

When E.D. Morel was imprisoned on a trumped up charge, Hardyman wrote letters of encouragement to him, and after Hardyman was killed it was discovered that he had left £50 in his will to help Morel continue his political career (Morel went on to defeat Winston Churchill in Dundee in 1922).[5]

In the sound archive of the Imperial War Museum, the battalion bombing officer, Cecil Tubbs, recorded that 'He was a great character. I loved him but some people, including the Brigadier, hated him. He always said what he thought and it was difficult to fault him. I know he was offered two constituencies in Edinburgh for the next election. The Brigadier found him playing chess on the eve of an assault, and was furious – but he said everything was organised and he knew exactly what he was going to do.'[6]

Hardyman was a committed Christian – and a poet. After the war his friends published a collection of his poems which were published under the title *A Challenge*. It is still in print, and although not in the same category as Owen and Sassoon it gives a vivid picture of the young Hardyman.

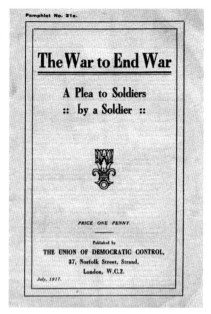

The UDC published several pamphlets. One of which may have been written by Hardyman.

> LORD JESUS of the trenches,
> Calm 'midst the bursting shell.
> We met with Thee in Flanders,
> We walked with Thee in Hell;
> O'er Duty's blood-soaked tillage
> We strewed our glorious;
> Yes, we indeed have known Thee
> For us the Cross is Truth.

No doubt he and Hardy had much to talk about and it is extremely sad that we can now only speculate what they discussed.

*   *   *

The term Service Battalions is applied to the New Armies of volunteers raised in the early months of the war when Lord Kitchener was Secretary of State for War. The 8th Lincolns were originally all volunteers and were formed in September 1914. At first there were no uniforms and very few rifles. 'At Lincoln, so many men volunteered that they were lined up in fours on the parade ground and a sergeant walked down the ranks and counted out 1,000 men. When he had enough, he stopped, put his hand out and said: "Every man this side of me turn right. You are now the 8th Lincolns".'[7]

When Theodore Hardy joined his battalions it was in the hardest winter on record since 1880/81. The military correspondent of *The Times* reported that the Household Cavalry infantry battalion had had heavy losses from frostbite.[8] Field Marshal Sir Douglas Haig, Commander-in-Chief of the British Armies, recorded 25 degrees of frost in his diary, and noted that at Boulogne the sands were all frozen as the tide went back.[9]

Hardy joined with a large draft of new recruits that were needed to replace losses suffered during four and a half months of the dreadful Somme offensive. Between 1 July and 20 November 1916, the Lincolns lost 40 officers and over 100 NCOs. On the first day of the offensive casualties amounted to 251 at Fricourt in what was regarded as one of the more successful parts of the offensive. In the last week, up to 20 November, it was 175. This has to be set against a normal battalion strength of 36 officers and just under 1,000 men.[10]

Heavy losses were not a new experience. The 8th Lincolns, a Volunteer Service Battalion formed as part of Kitchener's New Army in the autumn

The winter of 1916/17. A back area of the Somme.

of 1914, first arrived in France on 10 September 1915, with a strength of 28 officers and 995 men. After a two week forced march, they were pitched into the Battle of Loos without any previous trench or combat experience. Within a few short hours, they lost 22 officers and 471 men, including their commanding officer.

Early in the New Year of 1917, Hardy was to get his first experience of life in the front line. His battalion entered the trenches at Neuve Chapelle, only a few miles north of where they had suffered such terrible losses at Loos, and itself the scene of a disastrous British offensive in March 1915.

The line ran near the waterlogged meadows of the Lys Valley – now hard, frozen and bleak as the east wind blew across the flat landscape. To the south lay the slag heaps and pit heads of the coalfield around Loos.

After two years of war, the conflict had come near to stalemate with both sides entrenched in a 'ditch across Europe' stretching from the Channel ports to the Swiss border. A trench newspaper, *The Wipers Times,* described the scene: 'Take a wilderness of ruin, spread with mud quite six feet deep, In

A letter from Captain F. Brown, Adjutant of the 8th Lincolns, recalling Theodore Hardy's arrival at the front. The letter was written fifty years on after publicity in the Daily Telegraph about Hardy's medals being presented to the Chaplains' Department at Bagshot.

The Double Crassier (Coal slagheaps, near Lens). View from the British trenches where Hardy performed his first act of heroism in January 1917.

this mud now cut some channels, then you have the line we keep. Get a lot of Huns and plant them, in a ditch across the way; Now you have war in the making, as waged from day to day.'[11]

Bernard Martin, a subaltern in the war, gives a vivid description of what Hardy was to experience when he moved up into the line. 'The front trench, where we lived ... was irregular in depth and width. It had suffered many direct hits by enemy shells and was more or less always under repair. Somehow I had assumed continuous gunfire at the Front, shells falling on the trenches all day, and of course a regular rattle of rifle and machine gun fire. It was almost disquieting to be told there were long periods when war was silent. But the front trench usually had a daily concentrated strafe lasting perhaps thirty minutes and some intermittent shelling at Dawn-Stand-To and Dusk-Stand-To when all troops were on duty, an hour each period. A communication trench connected the front trench with Battalion H.Q., a small group of dug-outs four or five hundred yards back, where Colonel, Second-in-Command and Adjutant lived. All supplies, rations and relieving troops used this communication trench under cover of darkness. I was told ... "Seems a natural impulse to take a quick look over the trench parapet in daylight … but an impulse to resist. In most parts of the line it would be risky, hereabouts fatal. Very active snipers over the way".'[12]

The poet Robert Graves, answering the question 'What was it like?', wrote, 'Our homes, our privies, our graveyards; like air-raid shelters dug in a muddy field, fenced by a tangle of rusty wire, surrounded by enormous craters, subjected not only to an incessant air-raid of varying intensity, but to constant surprise attacks by professional killers, and without any protection against flooding in times of rain. And the smells: of corpses, latrine buckets, rotting sandbags, human sweat, chloride of lime, frying bacon. And the sounds; clatter of working parties, rattle of dixie-lids, squeak of rats; laughter and curses and, at sunrise and sunset the cry of 'Stand-to."[13]

Private Jimmy Watson of the 8th Lincolns remembered the cold, the lice and the impossibility of getting anything dry. He also remembered Theodore Hardy, 'He was always with us. He was always in the front line.'[14]

At first the officers and the men took very little notice of Hardy, though when he visited them in the trenches during the day they were always kind to him. Hardy wondered whether if he were to sleep in the day time and visit the trenches at night he might not be more sympathetically received. Accordingly, after his evening meal he made his way to the front line with a knapsack filled with sweets and cigarettes and in a letter to his brother reported that he was 'heartily welcomed and got to know the men well.'[15]

Another memory of Hardy's first few days came from Major General Bruce-Williams, Commander of the 63rd Infantry Brigade, the Brigade to which the Lincolns and Somersets were attached. 'My first introduction to him was at Lestrem in January 1917, when I attended the Battalion Church parade in a field near the village. Mr. Hardy

Major General Sir Hugh Bruce-Williams (1865–1942).

took the service, and I still firmly believe he was asleep standing when saying some of the psalms and prayers. He had most probably been up all night in the trenches! He thought nothing of spending the night in the trenches and waking up in the morning in time to take early Communion and several subsequent parade services.'[16]

Fatigue may also explain an incident at this time recalled by a young lieutenant (C. R. Madden) who himself went on to win the Military Cross, 'I can well remember an incident which occurred on a Sunday when we were out of the line and billeted in a village. The Padre and myself were quartered in the same room and I found him sitting on his bed in great distress and even tears. I discovered the cause to be that his voluntary service had only been attended by some twenty men. "What do I do that is wrong?" he said. "What is my mistake?" This was typical of his attitude, and an index to his devotion to duty.'[17]

The truth is probably that the men were too weary to do anything other than sleep, and that Hardy's own weariness had led to undue introspection and depression. The mood soon passed; if the men wouldn't or couldn't come to him, he would go to them, and not necessarily with words but with actions. He told his Divisional Chaplain, Geoffrey Vallings, that he had decided to live always and entirely with the officers and men in the line whatever the discomforts and dangers, and concluded, 'It is the life which tells; without that preaching is of no use'.[18]

Within days of this conversation, Vallings witnessed the first of a number of 'Hardy incidents' – the rescue of a wounded man in the shadow of the notorious Double Crassier near Lens. The Double Crassier consisted of two parallel slagheaps of coal waste running at right angles from the German line to the British line across no man's land. It began at ground level in the German line and rose in height to sixty feet, ending immediately in front of the British line – allowing the Germans to see directly into the British trenches from an observation post. The British countered this with a one hundred step trench up to a short cross trench within yards of the German observation post. Both sides could hear each other talking, and exceptional precautions had to be taken in a most exposed and dangerous position. It was here that Hardy's first recorded act of heroism took place.

Geoffrey Vallings recalled, 'Two officers, on their way up the trenches, heard groanings and cries for aid, and at last discovered a man lying in the open beyond the parados. He had trusted to the fog, and been sniped. He was got into some sort of shelter and bandaged, but it was impossible to do more as they were in full view from the Double Crassier; and as the trench was almost up to the knees in mud, there was no use in attempting to move anyone along it. Word was taken to the nearest medical aid post, and it was arranged for stretcher bearers to carry him down over the open after darkness had fallen. The man belonged to the Somersets, who had just been relieved that day, and with whom Hardy had come out. When the latter heard of the circumstances nothing would satisfy him but to go up at once, though he sorely needed rest, and though the state of the trenches made walking a very severe strain, and further, he was assured everything possible had been done. I called him an obstinate old man, but I loved him for it. In the salient on more than one occasion he did the same sort of thing when he was absolutely worn out, and only his heroic spirit enabled him to carry on.'[19]

The battalion ended a two month spell of trench duty in mid-March, and began training for the expected spring offensive. For Theodore Hardy it was a chance to use his favourite mode of transport – a bicycle – and delight of delights, an opportunity to see his daughter Elizabeth who was a VAD (Voluntary Aid) Red Cross nurse based at the Queen Alexandra Hospital in Dunkirk. It was the second day of spring. The joy they shared in each other's company is evident from the letter they wrote together to William in Egypt.

Elizabeth began:

'Dear Will, This is being written in a tea shop (of course) in a dear little old town a few miles away from my work. I am having the day off and spending it with – guess who – the padre of the 8th Lincolns & Somersets. We only wish you were here. Otherwise the expedition is very like the one we went to Hawkshead nearly a year ago. Father turned up suddenly this morning & I was given the day off. He looks very well – the meat n'est-ce pas?'

Having had his vegetarian leg pulled, her father takes over the letter… 'Not a bit of it, though I am still degenerate & rather like it, to tell the truth. I had a good bicycle ride to get here, more than 90 kilos & most of the time

'Dear Will,

   This is being written in a tea shop (of course) in a dear little old town a few miles away from my work. I am having the day off and spending it with — guess who — the padre of the 8th Lincolns & Somersets. We only wish you were here. Otherwise the expedition is very like the one we went to Hawkshead nearly a year ago. Father turned up suddenly this morning & I was given the day off. He looks very well — the meat n'est-ce pas?'

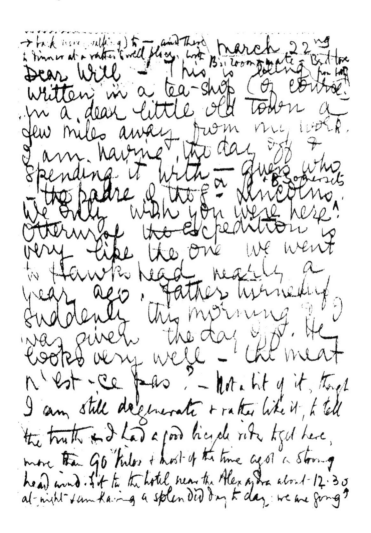

'I am still degenerate and rather like it, to tell the truth.'
Elizabeth and her father write to William in March, 1917.

'I am still degenerate and rather like it, to tell the truth.' Elizabeth and her father write to William in March, 1917.

against a strong head wind. Got to the Alexandra about 12.30 at night. I am having a splendid day today: We are going back now (walking) to ——— and there to dinner at a rather swell place, with bathrooms and water – Best love from both.'[20]

One can only speculate at the thoughts of this 53-year-old little cleric as he cycled the 60 miles across northern France to see his much loved daughter. But of one thing there can be little doubt, it must have seemed like Heaven on Earth to have had a hot bath and dinner in a 'swell place' after two months of ice, mud, bullets and death in the trenches.

Appendix: Theodore Hardy's Journeys on the Western Front: An Overview

This appendix contains a day by day calendar following Theodore Bayley Hardy's movements on the Western Front from the day he joined the 8th (Service) Battalion of the Lincolnshire Regiment and the 8th (Service)

Officers of the 8th Battalion, the Lincolnshire Regiment, taken in January 1919. Lieut-Colonel A. T. Hitch, D.S.O is centre, front row. Colonel Hitch was to write of Theodore Hardy: 'What his loss has meant to us is more than I can express, but his name will always be recalled with reverence, and to those of us who knew him really intimately, a great blank has appeared in our daily lives.'

Battalion of the Somerset Light Infantry at Sarton in the Pas-de-Calais in December 1916, to the day he was wounded on the bridge over the River Selle at Briastre in October 1918.

It is based on a small booklet that was produced after the war by Lieutenant Colonel Arthur Tyler Hitch DSO, the last commanding officer of the 8th Lincolns.[21] The Colonel produced the booklet at his own expense, describing it as 'a small memento, in the hope it may be of some value to all members of the Battalion, past and present. Its chief purpose is to wish the best of luck to all who have served in the Battalion, speedy promotion to those staying in the Army, and happiness and success to those who are resuming civilian life.' The colonel's booklet consisted of an abridged form of the official Battalion War Diary... and everywhere the 8th Lincolns went, they were accompanied by the 8th Somerset Light Infantry.

Colonel Hitch's booklet begins with sobering statistics revealing the appalling casualties suffered by a typical Kitchener Battalion, initially made up of volunteers, but increasingly of conscripts after 1916.

8th (Service) Battalion, the Lincolnshire Regiment

Strength of Battalion, 10 September 1915	28 officers	995 other ranks
Strength of Battalion, 11 November 1918	36 officers	782 other ranks
Total Battle Casualties	103 officers	2,841 other ranks
Total Members of Battalion	200 officers	4,700 other ranks

Within days of their arrival in France, and after a two-night forced march from Boulogne, the inexperienced Lincolns were thrown into the Battle of Loos. They suffered terrible casualties, losing 22 officers and 471 other ranks. The Loos debacle led to the replacement of Sir John French by Sir Douglas Haig as Commander in Chief of the British Expeditionary Force. As the battalions slowly recovered and assimilated new reinforcements, there followed a series of trench duties in Flanders and northern France around Armentières and in the area of the River Lys. The two battalions were involved in the beginning and the end of the Battle of the Somme. On 1 July 1916, the 8th Lincolns went over the top near Fricourt. They suffered 251 casualties, which was relatively light compared to many other Kitchener battalions. In an action at the very end of the Somme campaign in mid-

November, near the River Ancre, they suffered 175 casualties. In between these actions there was the daily loss of individual soldiers when they were in the trenches.

Theodore Hardy first met his two battalions at Sarton. The Lincolns had just returned after a tour in the trenches that had been recently captured by the Royal Naval Division on the River Ancre near Martinsart Wood. Colonel Hitch's abbreviated war diary tracks Hardy's movements over the next two years. It gives an indication of the vast effort and distances Theodore Hardy had to cover with them.

A reader with a modern Michelin road map of northern France and Flanders in Belgium will be able to track Hardy's movements. Whilst he was provided with a horse he preferred to march with the men and the junior officers.

1916

Dec 1	Arrived in billets in Sarton, marching via Acheux. Rev T.B. Hardy joined the battalion.
Dec 18	Billeted in La Perrière, having marched via Mézerolles, Conchy, Huclier and Amettes.
Dec 31	Battalion moved to billets in Vieille Chapelle

1917

Jan 1	Billets in Vieille Chapelle
Jan 8	Trenches in Neuve Chapelle sector. Period of trench duty. Billets in Locon, Béthune, Magingarbe areas.
Mar 4	Battalion marched to Boerecq via Robecq and Béthune.
Mar 10	Billets in Neuville-au-Cornet, moving via Tangry. Period of training.
April 8	Moved to Arras area, billeting one night at Duisan
April 9–13	Battalion in action at Arras.
April 14–23	Billets in Beaufort
April 23–29	Battalion in action at Arras. Casualties: 8 officers, 516 other ranks.
April 30	Battalion in billets at Beaufort
May 21	Battalion moved to Arras via Simencourt and Dainville
June 1	Battalion moved to Beaufort by bus.

June 7	Marched into Fruges, having billeted for one night each in Huchin and Croisette.
June 9	Moved to Radinghem and bivouacked.
June 25	Marched to Brulooze via Rely, Steenbecque and Caëstre.
June 29	Took over trenches in Wytschaete sector. Battalion headquarters at Zero Wood.
July 2	Camp at Mount Kemmel. Period of trench duty in same sector.
July 31	Attack on Rifle Farm. Casualties: 7 officers, 170 other ranks.
August 1	Relieved by 13th Rifle Brigade; night at Kemmel Hill.
August 2	Moved to reserve area near Bailleul.
August 8	Chinese Wall
August 15	Relieved 11th East Lancashire Regiment in Denys Wood and Green Wood Sector.
August 22	Chinese Wall
August 26	Reserve area, Westoutre
August 29	Bois Confluent
Sept 2	Relieved 4th Middlesex Regiment in Hollebeke sector

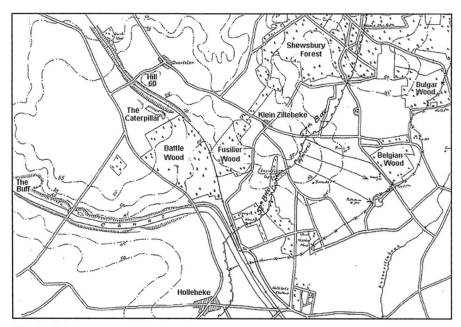

The Hollebeke sector of Flanders below the Menin Road. Hill 60 top left, Shrewsbury Forest top right.

Sept 7	Rossignol Wood (Flanders)
Sept 10	Reserve area, Berthen
Sept 27	Battalion moved into support in Shrewsbury Forest
Oct 1	Front line. Battalion HQ at Het Papotje Farm
Oct 4	Attack on Jute Cotts, Bury Cott. Casualties: 8 officers, 181 other ranks
Oct 6	Relieved by 6th Bedfordshire. Withdrew to Kemmel Hill camp
Oct 10	Relieved 10 Loyal North Lancs. Tower Hamlets sector.
Oct 15	Stafford Camp
Oct 21	Reserve area around Strazeele and Merris.
Nov 10	Moved to Bois-Carre, spending night at Dranoutre en route.
Nov 17	Murrumbidgee Camp.
Nov 25	Relieved 10 Royal Fusiliers in Hollebeke sector.
Dec 5	Spoilbank Tunnels
Dec 13	Murrumbidgee Camp
Dec 22	Relieved 13 Rifle Brigade in King's Castle sector.
Dec 29	Relieved by 11 Royal Warwicks. Withdrew to Tournai Camp.

1918

Jan 5	Murrumbidgee Camp
Jan 11	Mic-Mac Camp
Jan 21	Moved by train to Wallon-Cappel. Period of training.
Feb 15	Relieved 7 Duke of Cornwall's Light Infantry in Tower Hamlets sector having spent one night each at Strazeele & Foresters Camp.
Feb 21	Scottish Wood Camp.
Feb 23	Canada Tunnels
Feb 25	Relieved 4 Middlesex in Dumbarton Wood sector. Duty & reliefs
Mar 27	Proceeded by bus to Flêtre.
Mar 29	Proceeded by train from Caëstre to Pas area.
Mar 31	Marched to Hénu.
April 1	Relieved 5 KOYLI in Gommecourt sector.
April 5	Attack on Rossignol Wood. Casualties: officers 5, other ranks 193

April 6	Relieved by 13 Rifle Brigade. Support area in Gommecourt.
April 15	Billets at Hénu
April 16	Camp at Authie Wood
April 23	Support area at Gommecourt
April 27	Front line south of Bucquoy
May 1	Reserve at Essarts
May 5	Valley Camp, Souastre
May 9	Bucquoy
May 16	Camp in Bois du Warnimont
May 24	Relieved 2nd Canterbury (New Zealand) at Bus les Artois
May 30	Returned to billets in Authie.
June 5	Embussed at 9.30 pm to go south to French Army.
June 6	Arrived Fourdrinoy at 9.00 am
June 10	Moved to billets in Loeuilly by French busses.
June 15	Moved to Oresmaux, and finally Rumigny.
June 21	Entrained at Prouzel and returned to Pas area, Billets in Couin.
June 25	Support trenches at Essarts.
July 1	Relieved 4 Middlesex in Ablainzeville sector.
July 7	Souastre and Chateau de la Haie Switch.
July 10	Support trenches at La Brayelle.
July 13	Ablainzeville sector
July 17	Close support in Pigeon Wood sector
July 21	Bucquoy-Biez Wood sector
July 26	Valley Camp Souastre
July 29	Support trenches at La Brayelle.
Aug 2	Ablainzeville sector
Aug 8	Support area at Essarts
Aug 13	Bucquoy sector
Aug 17	Souastre and Chateau Switch
Aug 19	Support area, Pigeon Wood
Aug 20	Battalion moved to assembly positions
Aug 23	Beginning of final offensive. Attack on Bucquoy and Ablainzeville
Aug 23	Capture of Achiet-le-Grand and Bihucourt
Aug 24	Capture of Biefvillers

Aug 25	Capture of Bapaume. Casualties: officers 5, other ranks 172
Aug 26	Withdrew to Achiet-le-Petit
Sep 3	Moved to Beugny
Sep 5	Relieved 1 Hertfordshires. At Havrincourt Wood.
Sep 11	Relieved by 42nd Division. Withdrew to Lebucquière.
Sep 16	Reserve trenches near the Spoilbank
Sep 22	Camp at Thilloy.
Oct 1	Battalion moved to Gouzeaucourt Wood.
Oct 6	Marched through Gouzeaucourt to trenches near Gonnelieu.
Oct 8	Marched to Slate Copse near Vauchelles. Advanced to line in front of Briseaux Wood at dusk.
Oct 9	Advanced to Haucourt.
Oct 10	Advanced by Ligny Caudry and Audencourt to west bank of River Selle.
Oct 11	Rev T.B. Hardy VC DSO MC fatally wounded whilst visiting advanced platoons on east bank of River Selle.
Oct 12	Withdrew to billets at Caudry.
Oct	Casualties 8–12 October: officers 7, other ranks 86.

Over the next four weeks the battalion had one more spell of trench duty, and A Company launched one raid at Ghissignies.

Nov 11	News received at 1.00 am by wireless from Eiffel Tower of imminent signature of Armistice. Battalion marched to billets at Caudry.

Armistice signed.

Dec 20	Demobilisation commenced.

The remaining cadre of the battalions stayed in Charleroi until 14 April 1919. The cadre then left by train for Antwerp where they sailed to England for final dispersal.

List of Commanding Officers
8th (Service) Battalion, Lincolnshire Regiment

Lt Col H.E. Walters 9/9/15 to 26/9/15 Missing

Major H. Pattinson (temporary command) to 10/10/15

Major R.H. Wilson 10/10/15 to 18/11/15 Wounded

Lt Col R.H. Johnson 18/11/15 to 9/12/16 Transfer/England

Lt Col E.A. Cameron (Brig Gen) 9/12/16 to 14/1/17 Wounded

Major D. Davies Evans 14/1/17 to 12/2/17 Return, 8 SLI

Lt Col Thomas Astley Cubitt CMG DSO 12/2/17 to 31/3/17 Brig Gen

Major F.W. Greatwood 1/4/17 to 10/4/17 Wounded

Major H. Hussey 10/4/17 to 16/4/17 Return, 8 SLI

Lt Col D. Davies Evans 6/4/17 to 10/10/17 To England

Lt Col R.T. St John 10/10/17 to 29/1/18

Major R.M. Phelips 29/1/18 to 28/2/18

Lt Col W.I. Webb Bowen DSO 1/3/18 to 8/3/18 to 12 Brigade

Major R.M. Phelips 8/3/18 to 25/3/18

Lt Col W.I. Webb Bowen DSO 25/3/18 to 31/3/18 Brigadier General 112 Brigade

Major R.M. Phelips 1/4/18 to 4/6/18

Lt Col A.T. Hitch DSO 4/6/18 to 15/4/19

Shortly after Hardy joined the 8th Lincolns, it came under the command of Thomas Astley Cubitt for seven weeks in February and March 1917. It must have been a somewhat disturbing experience and one must suppose that Hardy kept out of his way. He would certainly not have approved of his choice of language. Cubitt later commanded the 38th Division and in the 1930s became the Governor of Bermuda.

In appearance General Cubitt bore a resemblance to a certain General Melchett in the *Blackadder* series. He was described as 'a very large and fierce-looking Major General, with two rows of ribbons, and a

General Sir Thomas Astley Cubitt CMG DSO (1871–1939). CO 8th Lincolns, February/March 1917.

gleam in his eye,' who proceeded to interrogate a subaltern about the exact type and position of his unit's trench latrines, apparently something of a pet topic.[22] A 'fire-eater with a marvellous flow of language,'[23] it was Cubitt's manner of speech, more than anything else, which made an impact on his contemporaries; a front-line officer in 1918 described watching him, during the October offensive, clearing a traffic jam with merely 'a magnificent gush of language'.[24] A colleague from his early days in the artillery described him as a 'perpetual joy to the soldier's world... because of his picturesque language, which never gave offence because it was so absolutely natural and so aptly fitted the occasion,'[25] but under some circumstances it proved less suitable. Following a failed raid in 1918, he visited the offending battalion and harangued the officers collectively for some time, before demanding that they 'damn well had to do the raid over again, and damn well see that [they] made a proper job of it, or, by God, damn well go on raiding until [they] damn well did.'[26] To the officers on the receiving end, already tired and dissatisfied, this was seen as a 'contemptible exhibition' for a senior officer to make.[27]

Chapter Eight

Over the Top: Arras, April 1917

"Good morning, Good morning!" the General said,
When we met him last week on our way to the line.
Now the soldiers he smiled at are most of 'em dead,
And we're cursing his staff for incompetent swine.

"He's a cheery old card" grunted Harry to Jack
As they slogged up to Arras with rifle and pack …
But he did for them both by his plan of attack.

The General, Siegfried Sassoon.

The weary stalemate continued throughout the Western Front during the first four months of Theodore Hardy's service there, but elsewhere profound and significant changes had taken place away from the Western Front.

Seven days before the padre of the 8th Lincolns and his daughter enjoyed tea together, the Tsar of all the Russias was deposed. It was to be only a matter of months before Russia left the war completely. Two weeks later America entered the war, provoked by unrestricted U-boat warfare and an astonishing German effort to incite Mexico to attack the USA.

In Britain, the mercurial and devious Lloyd George had replaced the exhausted Asquith as Prime Minister. The French Government meanwhile had replaced their commander-in-chief, the ponderous, taciturn 'Papa' Joffre, with the aggressive and over self-confident Nivelle. Nivelle's boast, 'We have the formula', combined with his fluent English, made an immediate appeal to Lloyd George. Relations between the British Prime Minister and his own commander-in-chief, Haig, were marked by mutual suspicion, distrust and intrigue.

Lloyd George backed Nivelle's new plan for a massive French attack on a thirty mile front in the Champagne area, not only to take pressure off the British troops, but also to undermine Haig's authority. This was to be 'the decisive blow' which would win the war, according to Nivelle. On 9 April, a British attack to the north in the Arras area would act as a diversion. The French attack would commence on 16 April.

The Germans were fully aware of the French plans. They were also making preparations to fight a defensive war until such time as the U-boat campaign succeeded and fresh forces could be redeployed from the Russian front. A massive defence system (known as the 'Siegfried line' in Germany and the 'Hindenburg line' to the allies) was constructed from near Arras south to the Aisne. Throughout March the Germans quietly withdrew to this line. They destroyed and booby trapped an area twenty miles deep and sixty miles long between the existing front and the new defence line. They then waited for the Allies to attack.

The British response came in the Battle of Arras on 9 April 1917. The 8th Lincolns and 8th Somersets were part of the 37th Division and took the offensive from the centre of the city of Arras. Six other divisions attacked to the south, whilst ten divisions, including the Canadians, attacked to the north towards Vimy Ridge. In the north, the objective was to capture the heavily defended and strategically important Vimy Ridge. In the south, the intention was to turn the northern flank of the Hindenburg line and drive on to Cambrai.

The Lincolns and Somersets' immediate objective was Orange Hill. Theodore Hardy accompanied the attack, helping to set up the advanced dressing station at Feuchy Chapel on the Arras-Cambrai road. The building still stands and is now in the shadow of the motorway.

On Easter Monday, 9 April, the Lincolns and Somersets, their padre with them, went over the top. They knew nothing of the background intrigues or overall strategy. Their function was to do their duty and to capture Orange Hill. They assembled for the attack by way of sewers and wine storage tunnels of the ancient but by now battered town of Arras, so as not to be seen by the enemy. Each man carried half his own weight in equipment: rifle, bayonet, steel helmet, entrenching tool, full water bottle, groundsheet, two days' rations, three sandbags, 170 rounds of rifle ammunition, two Mills bombs, and a flare to assist reconnaissance

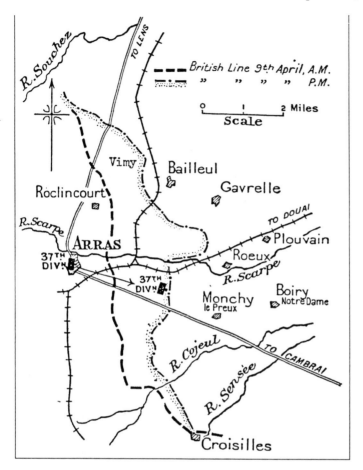

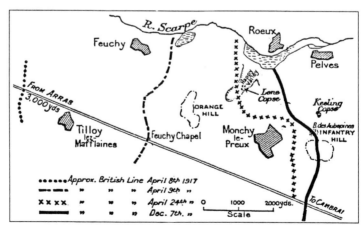

63rd Infantry Brigade (8th Lincolns, 8th Somersets, 10th Yorks & Lancs., 4th Middlesex) attacked along the northern edge of the Arras–Cambrai road.

aircraft. In view of this weight it was decided not to wear great coats. As soon as this decision was made, the snow and sleet began to fall. Three lines of German trenches lay between Arras and Feuchy Chapel. All were captured by troops of 12th Division during 9 April. 37th Division passed through during the day as a second wave, and by midnight the Lincolns and Somersets had captured Orange Hill. For the next three days they were to face fierce resistance as they gradually advanced and helped to capture Monchy-le-Preux. There were heavy casualties.

Siegfried Sassoon, who was wounded in the Arras offensive, writes of 'an emotional padre who was painfully aware that he could do nothing except stand about and feel sympathetic'.[1]

If Sassoon had been taken to Feuchy Chapel dressing station, literary history may have taken a different turn. Hardy at once got to work carrying the wounded on stretchers from the front. His ambulance class training at Kirkby Lonsdale was put to good effect. He made notes so as to write to the relatives of the dead and wounded. The men knew him and trusted him; his quiet courage gave them strength and calm, and when they asked for it he would quietly pray with them.

His colleague, Geoffrey Vallings, has a different story to Siegfried Sassoon, 'During the first Arras battle, April 9th, I directed [Hardy] to proceed with one of the medical officers who was to form an advanced dressing station within the German lines if the attack proved successful. Being with the A.D.M.S. when the location was chosen, I pushed on to select a further site and bearer posts. Late at night I returned to the position about one kilometre beyond Tilloy on the Arras to Cambrai road, and found Hardy had been continuously at work for about thirty-six hours, so I ordered him to bed. You must remember that always he would obey me, not merely because I was his senior in rank, but because we were practically the same age. He wrapped himself in a blanket and slept like a child in the corner of a ruined cellar. There is extant a photograph of the dressing station, in which Hardy is distinctly recognisable, but I was never able to procure one. It appeared, unless my memory betrays me, in either the *Daily Mirror* or *Sketch*.'[2]

The Imperial War Museum searched their photographic collection and found the photographs Mr Vallings was unable to obtain. Theodore Hardy gazes with intent concern at a wounded soldier carried by a British corporal and three German prisoners. In the foreground the dead await burial. Easter

Advanced dressing station, Feuchy Chapel. Theodore Hardy can be seen peering over the shoulder of a German prisoner and a British Corporal at a wounded man on a stretcher, 10 April 1917.

Monday was never like this in Hutton Roof, although Hardy must have pondered on the similarity with a hill at Golgotha.

At first, the battle gave an illusion of success. To the north the Canadians spectacularly stormed Vimy Ridge, and 37th Division achieved a penetration of five miles. Allenby, commanding the 3rd Army, believed the breakthrough

The 8th Lincolns in advanced trenches watch as cavalry move forward to attack Monchy-le-Preux.

had come and issued the order that he 'wishes all troops to understand that the 3rd Army is now pursuing a defeated enemy and that risks must be freely taken.'[3]

It didn't seem like that at the front, although Allenby, believing in the break through, sent in the cavalry. A Gordon Highlander watched them near Monchy-le-Preux: 'During a lull in the snowstorm an excited shout was raised that our cavalry were coming up! Sure enough, away behind us, moving quickly in extended order down the slope of Orange Hill, was line upon line of mounted men as far as we could see… It may have been a fine sight, but it was a wicked waste of men and horses, for the enemy immediately opened on them a hurricane of every kind of missile. If the cavalry advanced through us at a trot or canter, they came back at a gallop, including dismounted men and riderless horses… They left numbers of dead and wounded among us, but the horses seem to have suffered most, and for a while after we put bullets into poor brutes that were aimlessly limping about on three legs, or careering madly in their agony like one I saw with the whole of its muzzle blown away.'[4]

Such was Theodore Hardy's introduction to the Arras offensive. On the night of 12 April his battalion was relieved. By 14 April Allenby's determination to keep attacking, despite horrific losses and swirling snow in which units lost touch with each other, brought written protests from three of his Divisional Generals. Haig called a halt – until the weather improved nine days later and the offensive started again.

In the second phase of the battle it was the Somersets' turn to lead the offensive. Geoffrey Vallings again remembered Hardy's involvement and attitude. 'During the second Arras battle we attacked Greenland Hill, north of the Scarpe, between Gavrelle and the Roeux chemical works. On this occasion I insisted upon Hardy going back to the main dressing station at Haut Avesnes (five miles west of Arras), and I do not think he ever forgave me. I am satisfied that this probably saved his life. Our casualties were very severe, our positions exposed and several Commanding Officers were killed. Hardy would certainly have run risks in ministering to the wounded. One Chaplain was killed, another severely wounded, more than one besides had had very narrow escapes.

'Whenever possible, I relieved Hardy myself, and had simply to force him into bed, but so tired was he that he fell asleep directly his head touched the pillow. His ministrations were simply invaluable and his devotion absolutely untiring. On several occasions during our few days' rest before taking over the Wancourt to Guemappe line Hardy had several talks with me. He remonstrated over my sending him back, and pleaded to go forward in the next battle then impending. This gave me the deepest insight into his character. I argued with him that he owed a duty to myself, as his senior, and to his brother Chaplains; that if he were knocked out it would involve more work for us; that an older man with more experience was especially useful with a crowd of wounded and dying men, and that alive Hardy was much more valuable to everyone than a dead hero. He told me that he was a dreadful coward, but he felt sure that the forward area was the place for him, supplementing his plea with a great deal that I cannot repeat, and that I should spoil in the attempt. Here let me bear witness to the fact that Hardy's courage was no inability to appreciate danger, nor any sort of blind physical pluck, which nerves but few. Its source was complete confidence in his Master.

'He was never regardless or unconscious of danger, but his spirit rose supreme above it…

'I cannot reproduce it all except with more time than is at my disposal; indeed, probably I could not do so at all – it is beyond me altogether. But the faith and love were so intensely beautiful that at the close of one particular conversation, when his Brigade was already on the line of march, and we were talking with our horses' reins on our arms, I was unable to speak. I was in the presence of a saint, and the Master Himself was standing by. I never argued again.'

The Lincolns suffered terribly in the Arras offensive with 524 casualties – over half the battalion's strength. The Somersets suffered too. Their casualties included Colonel Scott who was killed at Greenland Hill on 23 April. Maitland Hardyman took over temporary command when Colonel Scott was hit – and was subsequently awarded the Military Cross.

The battle left 30,000 British and Empire soldiers dead and 128,000 wounded. Twelve months later, the ground gained over a month's hard fighting was lost in a few short hours.

The Lincoln and Somerset survivors return to Arras after the battle.

In the south, Nivelle's French offensive was a disastrous failure. Within days it ground to a halt with over 200,000 casualties. Mutinies erupted throughout the French Army. Nivelle was dismissed and Petain appointed to restore order, but the French were clearly in no condition to continue any sort of offensive action and it was unlikely that they could resist any major German attack. The initiative now rested with Haig. He was to make his move in Flanders… towards a place called Passchendaele.

Horse Ambulances wait to take away the wounded from the Advanced Dressing Station near Tilloy, 10th April, 1917. Hardy can be seen standing in front of the canvas shelter attached to the building.

'STUCK FAST IN THE MUD'
by Alexander Jamieson

Jamieson was a Captain (and Quarter Master) in the 10th York and Lancaster Regiment, one of four Battalions (along with the Lincolns, the Somersets and the 4th Middlesex) in the 63rd Infantry Brigade. The incident occurred at Oosttaverne: the same circumstances and to the north of the place in which Theodore Hardy was awarded the DSO. In this case there was a happier ending, the man survived. Jamieson wrote: 'The beginning of an awful experience! One of the 10th Service Battalion York and Lancaster Regiment got held fast by the mud and slime in a shell hole which flooded as he struggled. To haul him with ropes was impossible as he would have died. It took four nights hard work by the Pioneers to get him free. His comrade stood by him day and night under fire. He fed him by means of a long stick. When eventually saved both went delirious.'

'Stuck Fast in the Mud' by Alexander Jamieson. *Courtesy of Imperial War Museum*

WAITING FOR A MAN TO DIE
Wambeke, Flanders, Friday, 3 August 1917

*'Wherefore Christian was left to tumble in the Slough of Despond alone…
but could not get out because of the burden that was upon his back: but I
beheld in my dream, that a man came to him, whose name was Help.'*

Pilgrim's Progress, John Bunyan

Reverie

The mud stank in his nostrils and his whole body shivered with wet and
cold. The pain in his wrist kept him awake although he was at the very edge
of his endurance.

He was waiting for a man to die. It couldn't be long now. He knew now
what it must have been like at the foot of that Cross at Golgotha. 'Lord, now
lettest Thy Servant depart in peace.'

The rain had gone on and on it seemed for ever. Odd how the poppies cling
to life when everything else has surrendered. The roses must be out now in
the garden at Hutton Roof. I wonder what Elizabeth is doing? I wonder if
Will is coping with the heat in Alexandria? Is there still a world out there?

The man moved and groaned. He was up to his neck in the slime. 'It's all
right. I'm still here. I'll stay with you.'

He'd sat with Florence like this, but when he came back from the Church
she had gone. Waiting, waiting. Is it Thursday or Friday? It doesn't matter,
I suppose. What is time anyway? It's a puzzle how it goes so slowly and so
quickly. 'It's all right, I'm still here.'

Do you remember the smell of the juniper on the crag? We used to look at
the stars and realise how small we are. I hope Wilson is safe … 'The Son of
man must suffer many things, and be rejected of the elders and chief priests
and scribes, and be raised the third day' – 'It's all right. I'm still here. I'll
stay with you.'

I never knew it could be so cold in August. Do you remember the wind
in your face coming down Lupton Hill on the bike? We used to walk on the
crag in the rain, but it wasn't as cold as this.

'Come on, Padre. He's gone. You can't do any more. For goodness sake
you're cold. Let me rub your legs… Put this blanket round his shoulders…
Now come on, and keep your head down.'

'No, I must read the Burial Service. You can join in if you wish.' 'I am the resurrection and the life ...'

Much later they gave him a DSO – some people said it should have been a VC.

'Somehow, it didn't seem to matter and it was all rather embarrassing really. It wasn't much, was it? If anybody should have had a medal it was that young lad in the mud. He's dead and I'm still alive.'

Chapter Nine

A Place Called Passchendaele

'I died in Hell… They called it Passchendaele'
Memorial Tablet, Siegfried Sassoon

The third Battle of Ypres, better known as the Passchendaele offensive, lasted from 31 July to 10 November 1917. The British gained seven miles of Flemish slime and mud at the cost of at least 265,000 casualties. The defending Germans (who had lost 200,000) recaptured it all six months later.

What was to become known as the 'battle of the mud' was planned as a clean breakthrough to the Flanders coast. It turned into a battle of attrition where men drowned in shell holes filled with rain, and where horses and

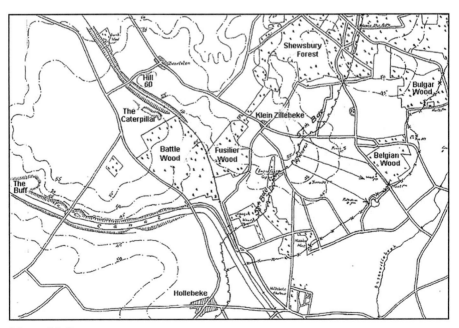

Map of Salient.

mules literally disappeared into craters of slime. In this hellish place Theodore Hardy was awarded the Distinguished Service Order and the Military Cross.

After their heavy losses at Arras, the 8th Lincolns had spent most of May and June in billets, integrating a new influx of conscripts. Towards the end of June they marched sixty miles north to the Ypres sector, taking over trenches near Wytschaete.

Wytschaete lay astride the Messines Ridge, captured from the Germans just three weeks before the arrival of the Lincolns. The capture of the Messines Ridge had been one of the few spectacular successes in an otherwise stalemate situation. Eight miles of German trench line had been mined from underground tunnels constructed over the previous two years. On 7 June, nineteen enormous explosions destroyed the trench system; the total charge of just under one million pounds of high explosive was heard in London. British troops captured and held on to the ridge. Hardy's mentor Geoffrey Studdert Kennedy was awarded the Military Cross in the subsequent German counter-attacks.

The seven week delay between the capture of Messines Ridge and the opening of the main offensive towards Passchendaele was to be of critical importance. It allowed the Germans to consolidate their defensive positions. Paradoxically, the delay was the result of Lloyd George's lack of faith in Haig's ability to undertake an offensive without heavy losses on the scale of the Somme. Lloyd George eventually agreed to the Passchendaele offensive with the pre-condition that it be discontinued if casualties were incommensurate with the ground gained. Having got his way, Haig went on to ignore this condition, convinced in his own mind that 'Germany is within 4 to 6 months of a date at which she will be unable to maintain the strength of her units in the field… Germany may well be forced to conclude peace on our terms before the end of the year.'[1]

For two weeks before the infantry attack due on 31 July, the Lincolns and Somersets, in their trenches east of Wytschaete, witnessed the heaviest British artillery bombardment yet on the German positions. Shells screamed ceaselessly overhead day and night from behind them whilst German artillery fired back.

The British bombardment was intended to destroy enemy positions, thus easing the task of the infantry when they went over the top. Yet it had the effect of turning the ground over which they were to attack into a muddy nightmare. It totally smashed the delicate system of pipes and dykes draining the low lying Flanders fields, and as the bombardment ceased the rain came down.

At 3.00 am on 31 July, Private Jimmy Watson of the 8th Lincolns remembers being given the tablespoon of rum by his Platoon Officer that always preceded going over the top, 'We always knew that was it when we were given the rum.' At 3.50 am whistles blew and they climbed out of the trenches. Hardy went with them. 'He always came with us,' said Private Watson.[2]

The fighting was confused, although by the end of the day, 'The line gained by 63rd Brigade on 31st July varied in depth from a few yards to 400 yards.'[3] 'Some stiff close-quarter fighting ensued, and heavy casualties were inflicted on the enemy, but the attackers were hard pressed.'[4]

'D Company of the Lincolns and a Company of the 4th Middlesex fought it out where they were until they were all either killed or wounded.'[5] The adjutant of the 8th Somersets described Theodore Hardy's response to the situation that night. 'About 11.00 pm … the Germans were shelling our position very heavily; about fifty or sixty had been killed and wounded at one spot. The night was pitch dark, the shelling about the worst I have ever known, and the crying of the wounded and dying such that I shall never forget. The heavy shelling went on all the night and until about 3.00 am next morning. Amid those terrible scenes that "Saint of God" remained the whole time, helping to bandage the wounds and to carry the wounded to a dressing station some 300 to 400 yards away, which was also being badly shelled. The next morning the shelling had abated, and, looking round to see what damage had been done, I saw a man on the ground some little way off. It was the Dear Old Padre. At first we thought he was dead, but no. He had worked all night until he was absolutely exhausted, and dropped down where he had been working. We woke him, wishing to take him back where he could have food and rest, but he insisted upon first burying those who had fallen during the night, and nothing would persuade him to leave until this was accomplished.'[6]

On the night of 1 August, the exhausted Lincolns and Somersets were relieved by the 13th Rifle Brigade. The Lincolns had suffered 177 casualties and the Somersets 155. They had two week's rest before re-joining the line. Yet after only one night's rest, the 13th Rifle Brigade discovered that one man had returned – a small elderly padre. Within a few hours they were to be grateful to him.

A staff captain remembered his arrival and gives us a vivid description: 'I was interviewing a driver, who had reported for orders, as to whether to unload some ammunition or to take it further forward, when a Padre approached me.

'I shall often think of a figure, with a waterproof sheet folded over his arms, standing at a little distance away in a shy, unobtrusive and almost apologetic manner.

'I may say in passing that one of Padre Hardy's particular characteristics, as I learnt later, was that he found it extremely difficult to find his way about, which added greatly to the distance covered by him, and consequently to the fatigue and difficulty of any task.

'"Would you be good enough," he said, "to tell me how to get up to the line?" I asked him if he had ever been up there before and gathered that he had, but he didn't seem to know where he was, and I hated to let him go without a guide, so suggested, as it was getting late, that he should stay, and have something to eat, and that we could give him shelter for the night in what was called the Dormitory, a large shelter with six bunks. This the Padre accepted: he said he should be up very early in the morning, and would make arrangements to go up to the line with one of the runners. I handed him over to one of the officers who was looking after the Divisional Ammunition Dump, and saw no more of him.

'This was most characteristic; he said not a word of his mission, but just quietly went to work. Next morning he went to the forward post, out into "No Man's Land", and remained there between thirty-six and forty-eight hours by the side of a soldier who had been bogged, and was three parts submerged in the mud. He fed him to keep him alive, and worked with others the whole of the following night trying to extricate him.'[7]

The reason for Theodore Hardy's return was that he couldn't forget what he had seen during the attack by the Lincolns and Somersets. He knew wounded men still lay trapped in the mud in no man's land. He could not abandon them. Lieutenant Colonel Challenor, the brigade commander, described the events in a letter to Mary Hardy after the war. 'In the attack on July 31st, the [63rd] Brigade attacked on the Wambeke Stream (East of Wytschaete) and the ground was in such a sodden condition that many men were buried up to their shoulders, and being under the close and accurate fire of the enemy, it was only possible to try and extricate them by night. For several nights after the action, Mr. Hardy assisted in extricating these poor fellows and in getting some food to them: on the third morning he was reported missing and could not be found for many hours. He was then found lying exhausted and asleep in a wet shell hole near the front line; so exacting had his labours been for the two previous nights he had collapsed from sheer fatigue.'[8]

Hardy had in fact stayed with a dying man during the day as well as the night, talking to him, encouraging him, feeding him and enduring constant sniper and machine-gun fire. He had, himself, suffered a broken wrist, but he would not abandon the man until death intervened. Much to Hardy's astonishment, he was awarded the DSO after this episode.

Oostaveme in the Passchendaele offensive. Here Theodore Hardy was awarded the DSO for staying with a dying man trapped in the mud of a shell hole. They were under enemy fire, yet despite Hardy's own broken wrist (shown top right) he stayed with the man for over 36 hours giving what comfort and support he could.

The citation was published in the *London Gazette*:

DISTINGUISHED SERVICE ORDER, REV. THEODORE BAYLEY HARDY,
London Gazette, published 18th October, 1917
London Gazette, details 7th March, 1918
Army Chaplains' Department, att'd 8th Battalion Lincolnshire Regiment

For conspicuous gallantry and devotion to duty in volunteering to go with a rescue party for some men who had been left stuck in the mud the previous night between the enemy's outpost line and our own. All the men except one were brought in. He then organised a party for the rescue of this man, and remained with it all night, though under rifle fire at close range, which killed one of the party. With his left arm in splints, owing to a broken wrist, and under the worst weather conditions, he crawled out with patrols to within seventy yards of the enemy and remained with wounded men under heavy fire.[9]

According to Geoffrey Vallings, the award would have been the Victoria Cross if sufficient eye witnesses could have been found. Hence, also, the delay from August.[10]

Despite all the horrors described in this chapter, the major British effort had been concentrated to the north of Hardy's position, above the Ypres to Menin road. Throughout August, Gough's Fifth Army had led the offensive to the north east of Ypres.

By 16 August, General Gough had had enough. 'The state of the ground was by this time frightful. The labour of bringing up supplies and ammunition, of moving or firing guns, which had often sunk up to their axles, was a fearful strain on the officers and men… When it came to the advance of the infantry for an attack, across water-logged shell holes, movement was so slow and fatiguing that only the shortest advances could be contemplated. In consequence I informed the Commander-in-Chief that tactical success was not possible… and advised that the attack should now be abandoned.'[11]

Haig would not accept this. According to Gough, 'He thought that he was killing a lot of Germans.'[12]

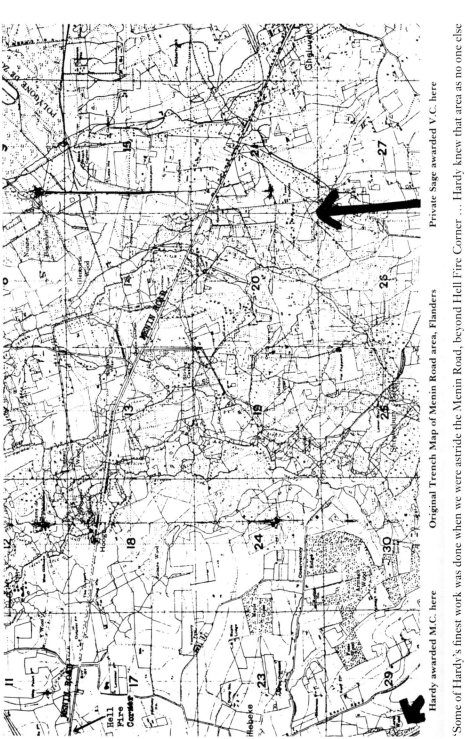

Hardy awarded M.C. here   Original Trench Map of Menin Road area, Flanders   Private Sage awarded V.C. here

'Some of Hardy's finest work was done when we were astride the Menin Road, beyond Hell Fire Corner … Hardy knew that area as no one else did, and it was very difficult to relieve him.' Geoffrey Vallings

However, by the end of August, Haig did decide to switch tactics, transferring the offensive further south from Gough to Plumer's Second Army. Now it would be the turn of Hardy's own two battalions' comrades to take the full impact of the offensive.

There was a three week pause throughout September as Plumer made completed preparations. He decided upon a more sophisticated limited number of short advances preceded by systematic and thorough shelling of the enemy positions with a creeping barrage. Attacks took place on 20 and 26 September. The Lincolns and Somersets were detailed to take part in the third attack on 4 October, towards Gheluvelt on the Menin Road in what became known as the Battle of Broodseinde. Then the rain began again.

In the attack of 4 October Private Thomas Sage of the 8th Somersets won the Victoria Cross at a sector known as Tower Hamlets to the south of the Menin Road. It was the supreme award for an act of supreme unselfishness, care for others and sheer spontaneous courage.

Tom Sage, a 35-year-old brewery worker from Tiverton, was a strong burly man used to heaving heavy beer barrels around. During the attack of 4 October he was in a shell hole with eight other men. One of them was shot by the enemy whilst in the act of throwing a Mills bomb. The live bomb, with

Chateau Wood, Flanders in the Autumn of 1917.

its pin out, fell back into the shell hole. Private Sage immediately used his great coat and threw himself on the bomb in an attempt to smother it and save the lives of his comrades. Amazingly, he survived, although he suffered severe wounds to his stomach and his face. Hardy helped to care for him at the advanced dressing station. He lived until 1945 and it's good to report that a plaque in Tom's memory was unveiled in Tiverton on the centenary of this heroic act, 4 October 2017. It was a privilege for me to accompany Tom's son to visit the site of his father's heroism back in 1991.

Private Thomas Henry Sage VC, 8th Somerset Light Infantry.

Geoffrey Vallings wrote of the Battle of Broodseinde, 'Some of Hardy's finest work was done when we were astride the Menin Road, beyond Hell

The mud of Passchendaele. It could take as many as eight men to move a stretcher. 'That Hardy is the finest chap I have ever seen; he is not content to go out with one squad of bearers, he goes out with all. By God, he deserves every decoration a man can win!' RAMC Corporal

Fire Corner … The Boche bombardments were terrific, possibly the worst in my own experience. Hardy knew that area as no one else did, and it was very difficult to relieve him. A Corporal in the RAMC said in my hearing, though without being aware of my presence, "That Hardy is the finest chap I have ever seen; he is not content to go out with one squad of bearers, he goes out with all. By God, he deserves every decoration a man can win." I may mention that in less than a week we lost over one hundred stretcher-bearers knocked out in one way or another.'[13]

Conditions were so appalling at the time, that it would sometimes take as many as eight men to carry one stretcher. For a man approaching his 54th birthday the physical demands must have been extremely punishing.

Within days Hardy was to win another award; this time the Military Cross. The event took place below the notorious Hill 60 as he was passing an artillery battery on his way, inevitably to the front. His friend and colleague Geoffrey Vallings was a witness and a participant to what happened: 'That Hardy was difficult to relieve was his own doing, as it was so impossible to find him. I had arranged to meet him at the Larch Wood tunnels. On my arrival a message was given to me that having had a good sleep he needed no relief, and had gone up the line. He had played this trick before, so I determined to follow and find him. Between the Canada Street and Larch Wood tunnels ran a light railway which we utilised for bringing down wounded on trucks. Hardy was coming down with two RAMC men in charge, when a man from a heavy battery not far away shouted that they had some severely injured. At the same moment the Boche opened an appalling bombardment. No other word will describe it, so you must excuse me saying it was absolute hell. However the job was done, though how anyone lived through it is a mystery to myself. The whole surface of the ground seemed to be shot away. Hardy's calm confidence was an inspiration. He received most deservedly the Military Cross, and the two other men the Medal. Over and over again his courageous example has nerved me to try and follow his lead, as to my knowledge it has many others.'[14]

Geoffrey Vallings' modesty stands out in this account. He took part in the rescue and was awarded the DSO for his actions.

The rubble that was Passchendaele village finally fell to the Canadians on 6 November. The following day Haig's chief of staff, General Lancelot Kiggell, paid his first visit to the combat zone. As his car lurched along the

Larch Wood and Canada Tunnels near Hill 60. Men look up from loading ammunition on to the light railway as a shell bursts on the ridge. Hardy was awarded the Military Cross here in October, 1917, for rescuing a group of severely wounded men under heavy artillery fire.

Menin Road, through the swampland, he became more and more agitated. Finally, he broke into tears and muttered, 'Good God, did we really send men to fight in that?' His companion, who had been through the campaign, replied, 'It's worse further up.'[15]

The mud turned to ice, but the 8th Lincolns and 8th Somersets continued trench duty in the Ypres sector throughout the winter.

In due course, Theodore Hardy was presented with his DSO and MC – much against his wishes, and indeed under protest. Lieutenant Colonel Hitch, Commanding Officer of the Lincolns, wrote, 'His retiring nature made it almost a penance to wear those ribbons which most of us would give our right arm for.'[16]

The Commander of the 63rd Infantry Brigade noticed that Hardy would 'place his left arm across his breast to hide his decorations when he was speaking to a soldier who himself had no such decoration.'[17]

Whenever his two battalions were relieved, Hardy would stay in the front line with the relieving battalion. He was 'handed over as a trench store.'[18]

Another memory of Theodore Hardy at this time comes from Sergeant Major Yaw, DCM of the Somersets. 'My job was to see that the Companies in the line were supplied with rations, water etc… and for that we used carrying

The mud of Passchendaele. Hardy visited men in trenches such as this every night without fail. He would help to carry rations and supplies. For a man of fifty-four, the physical stress must have been punishing.

parties… it was a difficult job as the ground was in such a condition, and very often men got stuck in the mud: Mr Hardy would come along and ask the time the party was going up, so that he would be able to go up with them.

'His main object in going was to help the men with their loads. Many a night has he carried up rations for a fellow who was not so able as the others. All he used to think about was helping others, never about himself. I often used to think he would be overdoing it, and be taken ill, as he was always on the go.

'After the rations had been handed over, he would proceed to the outpost line, where he would remain 'til it was too light to remain any longer. It was not very often he missed a post, which were very difficult to find, what with the conditions of the ground and the black nights: and he would always remain in the dangerous places the longest, cheering everybody up as he visited each post.'[19]

Seventy years later Private Jimmy Watson of the Lincolns still remembered the padre's nightly visits to the outposts. '"It's only me, boys," he would say. He would bring cigarettes and sweets and sometimes read to us. He would take letters back to post for us.'[20]

Jimmy Watson's commanding officer summed up the Lincolns' feelings about their 'Dear Old Padre': 'He was to all of us, who troubled to think a little below the surface, as nearly a true Christian as one can ever expect to meet on earth. He appealed to us all, both officers and men, by his absolute fearlessness, physical and moral, and by his simple sincerity and lack of cant or humbug. We loved him for his self-effacing devotion to duty.'[21]

On 21 March 1918, news came of a massive German attack to the south in the area of the Somme. The British 3rd and 5th Armies were forced back and were in a desperate situation. The Lincolns and Somersets were rushed south to reinforce the line. They found themselves in a familiar place at the northern end of the Somme in Gommecourt looking across no man's land to the shattered stumps of Rossignol Wood.

Chapter Ten

Waiting for a Boy to Live

Rossignol Wood, 5 April 1918

He was by himself now, the others had gone on and left him. His leg had felt numb at first, but by God it hurt and throbbed now – that is if you could call it a leg any more. His blood was mixing with the chalky mud – rather strange, he thought, just like putting jam in rice pudding at school.

School, now there's a thought; they'll be putting up the cricket nets again in Taunton. He'd wondered what it would be like to die, now he expected to find out, and truth to tell he didn't really mind. He felt very cold. He'd lain there since six o'clock in the morning, stuck in the wire.

'It's only me. Keep quiet and still. They're back in the pill box again.' He felt a tightening in his thigh as something was tied round it. Oh, my God, it throbs. He felt an arm round his shoulder and a coat being put over him. He must have been unconscious because it was nearly dark again.

'Ssh… Keep still. It's only me. I'm still here.'

He knew that voice. It was the padre, dear old Hardy. They talked in whispers. Rossignol Wood, it was called, a place for nightingales, but not tonight. The old man whispered to him how he used to go down to the Oval to watch W.G. bat when he was a schoolboy. 'Did he play cricket at school?' the old man asked. Yes, but the summer of 1917 seemed a long time ago. He didn't suppose he'd ever play cricket again with a leg like this. 'Course you will,' said the old man, 'Anyway you can't do worse than me… I always got a duck.'

'Oh God, God, God it hurts…'

His teeth chattered and his body was shaking. He could hear the Germans talking and laughing in the pillbox. They must have thought he was dead because they were only ten yards away. He couldn't understand what they said… only did Latin and Greek at school… 'Amo, Amas, Amat, Amamis, Amatis.'

'Shh... Keep quite still. I'm going to get help. I'll be back soon. You've done really well. Just hang on a bit longer.'

He felt an arm lift off his back, and the warmth of the old man's body go away from him. 'Oh, God it hurts, come back quickly.' He knew the old man would come back, that nothing, absolutely nothing, could stop him. Yes, he'd try to hang on a bit longer.

They did come back for him, the dear old padre and tough old Sergeant Radford, both old enough to be his father. He knew what the padre would say before he said it: 'It's only me.'

The sergeant snipped the wire with his cutters, deadening the sound with a cloth. It was like being a child again being carried back by these two old men. He'd tried to be brave, he really had. Then, he couldn't remember any more.

He heard later the sergeant got a DCM. Later again, he heard that when the colonel told the padre he was to get the VC, Hardy had replied, 'I really must protest.'

Rossignol Wood, Hebuterne. The remains of the German bunker on the southern corner of the wood, thought to be where Hardy, with Sergeant Radford, rescued the young officer and was awarded the VC.

Map showing Rossignol Wood.

Chapter Eleven

For Valour: The Victoria Cross

'What is courage but the inspiration of the Spirit.'

T.B. Hardy, July 1918

On 21 March 1918, the German Army made its supreme effort to win the war. The *Kaiserschlacht* (the Kaiser's battle) was one of the great turning points of the war, and involved more men than any other battle. The German survivors had stamped in their military service book: 'Grosse Schlacht in Frankerich' – 'The Great Battle in France'.

Like the British offensive in the summer of 1916, the first German attack came to the south of the British line in the area of the Somme.

The collapse of Russia in 1917 allowed Germany to transfer all her forces to the Western Front, allowing them to have superiority in numbers for the first time since the autumn of 1914. Ludendorff and the German High Command planned the attack with great care and in the minutest detail.

Their tactics were new and revolutionary, heralding the Blitzkrieg of 1940, and were remarkably effective. Strongpoints and areas of heavy resistance were to be bypassed and 'mopped-up' later; the line of least resistance was to be pursued and exploited. For the first time, the word 'stormtrooper' came into the language of warfare.

The attack dealt a devastating blow to the British, particularly to the 5th Army under the command of Hubert Gough. They were holding the most thinly defended part of the line to the south. For a few days it appeared as if the British Army could be defeated.

The 8th Lincolns, 8th Somersets and 4th Middlesex in the 63rd Brigade were rushed south by bus and train from Ypres, arriving at Gommecourt at the northern end of the Somme on 1 April.[1]

By this time Gough had been relieved of his command and the British were fighting a desperate rear-guard action. All the gains, and more, of 1916 had been lost, and the Lincolns found themselves in trenches last used nearly two years before.

The German effort ended on 5 April. They had gained over 1,000 square miles of territory, inflicting 160,000 casualties on the British (22,000 killed, and 63,000 wounded, with 75,000 taken prisoners of war).

The next German effort switched to the Northern Somme, the area in part defended by the 8th Lincolns and 8th Somersets (the 4th Middlesex in reserve). As the Germans were forming up ready for this thrust, it was decided that 37th Division (including the Lincolns and Somersets) would take part in a local pre-emptive strike in order to disorganise the enemy's attack. The strike was to take place early on the morning of 5 April, and Theodore Hardy was to play such a full part in events that day that he was to receive his first (of four) recommendations for the Victoria Cross.

The *Official History* of the Lincolnshire Regiment records details of the two battalions' attack:

On the 3rd April orders were issued for an attack on Rossignol Wood and the enemy's trenches west and south of it, the final objective being a sunken road south-west of the Wood and a short length of trench running eastwards from the eastern end of the Wood. This entailed on the Lincolnshire front the capture of Duck, Swan and Owl Trenches: Rossignol Wood, with Fish Alley and Roach Trench were in the area of the Somerset attack.

The night of the 4th/5th April was miserable in the extreme: rain fell and the inky darkness made the forming up operations difficult… Tanks had been detailed to assist in the attack, but they were unable to advance. At zero hour (5.30 am) therefore, the Lincolnshires advanced without their assistance.

Within fifty yards of the jumping-off line the right section suffered severely from machine-gun fire, and a similar experience befell the left platoon. Considerable resistance from the first objective (Duck Trench) met the attackers, and heavy fighting took place during which about one hundred Germans were taken prisoner and from sixty to ninety wounded. This objective was captured by 5.45 am. Considerable machine-gun fire from both flanks met the attack on the second objective (Swan Trench)… Having captured this line, heavy bombing became general on the right. The line was cleared with the exception of two strong points… and at 7.45 am this position was being consolidated.

'At about 9.00 am, lorries full of enemy troops were seen travelling towards Rossignol Wood, but the Lincolnshire's still maintained their position. At midday the enemy was reinforced and the position of the battalion was likely to become serious.

'At about 1.00 pm the enemy advanced and cut right into the battalion dividing it into two sections. "From this time", the record states, "we were overwhelmed and, owing to the lack of bombs, we withdrew in good order into our original front line".'[2]

As the battalions re-grouped and counted heads in their original line, there was no sign of Theodore Hardy. The padre was missing.

As dusk approached and speculation grew that the man they had called 'the unkillable' would not be returning, a small figure was seen coming out of the wood from amongst the enemy lines. He had spent the day lying within ten yards of an enemy machine-gun post comforting a wounded man and now had come back to ask for a volunteer to go with him to recover the man.

Sergeant George Radford promptly agreed to return into Rossignol Wood with Hardy. They crawled in silence to where the man lay. Although he was

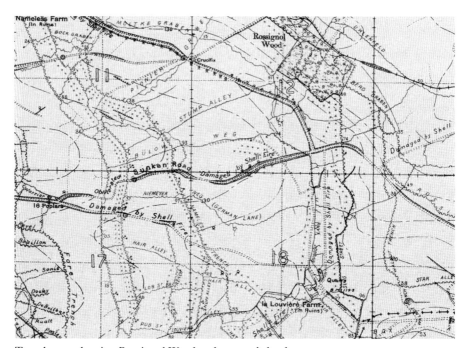

Trench map showing Rossignol Wood and no man's land.

Bucquoy, northern Somme area. Hardy's citation for the Victoria Cross includes mention of digging wounded out of a collapsing building in Bucquoy during the great German offensive in April, 1918.

too weak to stand, the sergeant and the padre somehow managed to get him back to the safety of the Somersets' trench.

Despite this ordeal, Hardy would not rest, as the citation continues, 'Throughout the day the enemy's artillery, machine-gun and trench-mortar fire was continuous, and caused many casualties. Notwithstanding, this very gallant chaplain was seen moving quietly amongst the men and tending the wounded, absolutely regardless of his personal safety.'[3]

The Brigadier, in his report on the day's events wrote: 'I consider that the behaviour of these battalions, which were composed largely of very young soldiers, was beyond all praise.' The Lincolns suffered 180 casualties, and the Somersets 161. Sergeant Radford who assisted Theodore Hardy was awarded the Distinguished Conduct Medal and other awards of the DSO, MC and DCM were made.

It was in the award of these other medals that Major General Bruce-Williams, the Commander of 37th Division, began to put together the facts leading to Theodore Hardy's award:

I met Mr. Hardy walking back from the trenches and hailed him, and I asked him whether he could give me evidence regarding acts of gallantry by NCO's and men during the counter-attack on April 5th, which finally stemmed the Germans' attempt to push their advantage after the British retreat to the Hebuterne-Bucquoy line.

He told me of several incidents, and I got him to name the men, and say what he saw them do. Having got the names out of him, he was always enthusiastic in his praise of the rank and file, I went then to interview the men whose names he had mentioned. Gradually out of these men I obtained and pieced together a story which proved that he, and nothing else, was really the inspiring spirit during a very hot period when the enemy's shelling was heavy to a degree. Then I made it my business to get the various statements recorded, and to see that they confirmed each other.

'The result was a V.C. for the Chaplain, who really *deserved it three times over.* I don't think Mr. Hardy ever realised that it was only out of his own mouth that I was able at last to get at the true facts of the case. For all the time he was so enthusiastic about the way other men behaved, and so keen that *their* gallantry should be recognised. Theirs was *nothing* to his.'[4]

The facts collected by General Bruce-Williams included events in the village of Bucquoy later in the month as well as the rescue on 5 April.

Although the main German effort was now transferred further north to Lens and to Flanders, the Gommecourt, Hébuterne and Bucquoy sector continued to be a most uncomfortable and difficult part of the line. Three more events took place on 25, 26 and 27 April in the ruined village of Bucquoy, and all resulted in the saving of life. To one mentioned in Hardy's vc citation, Colonel Challenor added details when he wrote to Mary Hardy: 'He followed an officer's night patrol without anyone being aware of the fact. This patrol was attacked, the officer was so seriously wounded that he probably would have bled to death. Fortunately for him, Mr. Hardy found him in the dark, and using his knife cord as a tourniquet, stopped the bleeding and got him into our lines safely.'[5]

Sergeant Major Yaw was an eye-witness. 'I remember him on one occasion; my company was holding the line, and the shelling was rather heavy; one of the posts, which was an old house, got blown in, and the men inside were buried underneath. Who should be first there but Mr. Hardy, who had already got some of them out by digging with his hands. I am sorry to say one poor fellow had to be left under the debris, having already been killed by the fall, and it was impossible to shift the other stuff, as the surrounding walls would have collapsed. Captain Hardy read the Funeral Service where he saved the others who would have been suffocated had he not been there, doing the work he loved, visiting the men.'[6]

The photograph in this chapter shows the condition of Bucquoy at this time. The CO of the 8th Lincolns remembered how difficult and dangerous the village was, and the part played by Hardy in the following weeks.

We were holding a part of the line which ran through the ruined village of Bucquoy – half the village was in our hands and half in German hands – and owing to the ruins of houses everywhere, it was an impossible task to construct anything in the way of a continuous trench. Our line consequently consisted of a series of posts garrisoned by about seven men each and lying, roughly, a hundred or a hundred and fifty yards apart; these posts were naturally made as inconspicuous as possible, and the location of these posts at night when visiting the men was a matter of the greatest difficulty owing to the ground between and all around them being a wilderness of ruined houses, hedges, fallen trees, and so on.

And yet when visiting these posts, we always met the Padre, either lying in a post chatting in undertones to the men, or making his way from one post to the next. He was more often than not by himself, although the Bosch was at that time quite enterprising, and would attempt to crawl round and rush one of the posts quite frequently.

'During this time, the Padre would not live at Company Headquarters, which was a few hundred yards behind the post line, but insisted on living at advanced Platoon Headquarters, which was in an old German dug-out about thirty yards behind the actual post line, and in a neighbourhood where trench mortar shells occasionally made things very unpleasant. It was the constant sharing of danger and hardships in the line which gave him his tremendous power with the men – a power he would never realise himself— and which endeared him so to us all.'[7]

On 11 July, it was formally announced in *The London Gazette* that the Reverend Theodore Bayley Hardy DSO MC, temporary chaplain to the forces 4th class, had been awarded the VC. The consensus of opinion in the two battalions was that 'he should have had it served up for breakfast every day'.

Citation for the award of the Victoria Cross

Reverend Theodore Bayley Hardy, D.S.O., M.C.
T/C.F. 4th Class, Army Chaplains' Department.
Attached 8th Battalion, Lincolnshire Regiment

For most conspicuous bravery and devotion to duty on many occasions. Although over 50 years of age he has, by his fearlessness, devotion to men of his battalion and quiet, unobtrusive manner, won the respect and admiration of the whole division.

His marvellous energy and endurance would be remarkable even in a very much younger man and his valour and devotion are exemplified in the following incidents.

An infantry patrol had gone out to attack a previously located enemy post in the ruins of a village, the Reverend Theodore Bayley Hardy, C.F., being then at company headquarters. Hearing firing, he followed the patrol and about 400 yards beyond our front line of posts, found an officer of the patrol dangerously wounded. He remained with the officer until he was able to get assistance to bring him in. During this time there was a great deal of firing and an enemy patrol actually penetrated between the spot at which the officer was lying and our front line and captured three of our men. On a second occasion when an enemy shell exploded in the middle of one of our posts, the Reverend T.B. Hardy at once made his way to the spot, despite shell and trench mortar fire which were going on at the time and set to work to extricate the buried men. He succeeded in getting out one man who had been completely buried. He then set to work to extricate a second man who was found to be dead.

During the whole of the time that he was digging out the men this chaplain was in great danger not only from shell fire but also because of the dangerous condition of the wall of the building, which had been hit by the shell which buried the men.

On a third occasion he displayed the greatest devotion to duty when our infantry, after a successful attack, were gradually forced back to their starting trench.

After it was believed that all our men had withdrawn from the wood Chaplain Hardy came out of it and on reaching the advanced post, asked the men to help him to get in a wounded man. Accompanied by a sergeant, he made his way to the spot where the man lay, within 10 yards of a pillbox which had been captured in the morning, but was subsequently recaptured and occupied by the enemy. The wounded man was too weak to stand, but between them the Chaplain and the sergeant eventually succeeded in getting him to our lines. Throughout the day the enemy's artillery, machine-gun and trench mortar fire was continuous and caused many casualties.

Notwithstanding, this very gallant chaplain was soon moving quietly amongst the men and tending the wounded absolutely regardless of his personal safety.

Dates of Acts of Bravery
5–25–26–27th April, 1918
London Gazette 11th July, 1918

Elizabeth had no sooner sent a telegram, 'Father awarded the V.C.' to William in Ismailia than she received an invitation to visit 3rd Army Headquarters at Frohen-le-Grande on 9 August. The King himself was to present her father with the supreme award, and she was to witness the ceremony. She described the events in a letter to William.

'It was to be a quiet and informal investiture. Father's V.C. was the first given. He had to stand in front of the King for about ten minutes listening to a full account of his deeds, looking perfectly miserable. A cinema apparatus was focussed on him all the time. He will appear in the London Picture House looking just like a schoolboy being scolded.

'Then the King put on him the Great Medal, and I was near enough to him to hear quite distinctly as he spoke general appreciative sentences; you can fancy how I felt all the time.'[8]

Elizabeth's warmth and pride in her 'naughty schoolboy' father shine through her account. This same warmth and pride can be seen as she watches on in the official photograph of the occasion.

The results of the 'cinema apparatus' have proved remarkably elusive. It is almost as if Hardy himself was trying to cover up his decorations again. The Imperial War Museum did indeed have film of the King's visit to France between 5 and 13 August. There is film of the King on 5, 6, 7, 8, 10, 11, 12 and 13 August; all catalogued with detailed descriptions, but of 9 August – nothing![9]

Nothing, that is, until at the very end of the catalogue is a bare description:

'Summary, see also reel 99, which consists of out-takes and additional material of the visit.' The film library curator kindly agreed to view

8 August 1918. Theodore Hardy receives the Victoria Cross from King George V at Frohen-le-Grand. His daughter Elizabeth watches on proudly in her nurse's uniform.

Painting of the scene by Terence Cuneo (1967).

these odds and ends – and found exactly four seconds of the King talking to Theodore Hardy and six seconds to Elizabeth. To the best of one's knowledge this brief four seconds is the only moving picture record of T. B. Hardy.

Terence Cuneo exercised some artistic licence. Frohen-le-Grand was nearly twenty miles behind the line, yet there is shell damage to a building more humble than reality; Hardy wears a helmet and his boots are dirty as if he had just come from the line.

Almost fifty years later, Elizabeth relived this day when her father's medals were presented to the Royal Army Chaplains' Department on permanent loan. She unveiled a painting of the scene by Terence Cuneo. She was apparently furious when she saw the dirty boots, exclaiming, 'I was up nearly all night polishing Father's boots.'[10]

A photograph of the ceremony appeared in the *Daily Telegraph* on 1 June 1967, and produced a number of letters from old comrades. Fred Mott, of the 8th Somersets remembered his 'gallant and beloved Chaplain' returning with the VC to find the battalion assembled in a barn at Souastre ready to

SOUASTRE (P.-4-C.) – Rue de Bienvillers.

The barn (right) at Souastre. It still stands today.

greet and cheer him – much to Mr Hardy's astonishment and embarrassment. Mr Mott wrote he had 'always remembered the way, when the Rev. Hardy left the barn, he held his hand over the decoration, and blessed a photograph of Fred's baby son.'[11]

The Imperial War Museum sound archive has a recording of a Somerset Sergeant recalling that when he congratulated the padre, saying, 'Well done, Sir', Hardy, clearly flustered, embarrassed and making a rapid exit, responded, 'It's all a mistake of the War Office' ... a statement straight out of the 'It's Only Me, boys' collection.[12]

Lieutenant Colonel John Hay Maitland Hardyman DSO MC MID.

The welcome in the barn at Souastre was held on 17 August. The moving spirit was the commanding officer 8th Somersets, Lieutenant Colonel John Hay Maitland Hardyman.

In a letter to Mary Hardy, Bishop Llewllyn Gwynne reported that when Colonel Hardyman first told Theodore Hardy of the recommendation for the Victoria Cross, Hardy protested. 'I knew nothing of what was going on in No-Man's Land while I was attending to an officer who had been seriously wounded on the wire entanglements. I really think I ought to put in a protest.'[13]

Hardyman no doubt smiled and shrewdly replied: 'All right, Padre, but if you do you will only be advertising yourself all the more.' Hardy reluctantly accepted this and allowed the recommendation to go forward.[14]

Six days before this conversation Hardyman's own conduct during a German attack earned him the DSO when he personally rallied the men and fought off the Germans.

Sadly, just a week after the welcome in the barn, Hardyman himself was killed. At the beginning of the British offensive north west of Bapaume he had gone forward in a tank to reconnoitre the ground. When he got out of the tank he was killed by shell fire.[15]

Miss Elizabeth Hardy, 80, with medals awarded to her late father, the Rev. Theodore Bayley Hardy, standing beside a painting showing King George V decorating him with the Victoria Cross in France in 1918. Miss Hardy appears as a Red Cross nurse in the Terence Cuneo painting, which was unveiled yesterday at the Royal Army Chaplains' Department Depot, Bagshot, Surrey. Photograph in the 'Daily Telegraph,' 1st June, 1967.

Theodore Hardy performed the Burial Service for his friend at Biefvillers near Bapaume. He himself had just over two months left to live.

The area where Theodore Hardy won his Victoria Cross has changed little over the years. Rossignol Wood still stands and the trees have now recovered. Wood anemones and cowslips grow in profusion in the wood. The German pillbox where Hardy stayed all day on the wire can still be found in the remains of the German trenches running along the south eastern edge of the wood. Piles of rusty old shells are still dumped on the edge of the road by farmers during their ploughing, and it is still possible to turn up bullets and bits of barbed wire in the fields round about. Hardy's was not the only VC awarded for action in Rossignol Wood. Three others were awarded for action there throughout the war.

It was in Achiet-le-Petit that Hardy was told of his appointment to be a chaplain to the King. The villages have now been rebuilt. A permanent sad reminder today are the numerous war cemeteries in the area. Sadly, Sergeant George Radford DCM was killed on 21 August 1918, just four days after Hardy returned to the battalion after being presented with his Victoria Cross. He lies in Gommecourt British Cemetery No 2. Hardy conducted the Burial Service.

Elizabeth Hardy had a remarkable life. She graduated from London University when very few women went on to further education. After her father's death, she left the Red Cross and took up a teaching post. She went on to become head of a girls' secondary school in Rangoon. During World War II she drove through Burma to India with girls packed into her car to narrowly escape capture by the Japanese. She then became head of a school in Bangalore before retiring to Cornwall.

William became a much loved GP in Croydon. His daughter, Patricia Hastings Hardy became secretary to the Anglican archbishop of Dublin, Church of Ireland. Patricia was a great source of information about her family and offered much help, kindness and hospitality to the author. It was a delight to discover the German concrete pillbox in Rossignol Wood in her company in 1989. Sadly, she died in 2005 and is buried with her parents. In April 1988, she presented her grandfather's New Testament to the Chaplains' Department for safe keeping and posterity.

Chapter Twelve

Mr Valiant-For-Truth

'For if the trumpet give an <u>uncertain sound</u>, who shall prepare himself to the battle' (I Corinthians 14.8). Passage marked by Hardy in his pocket New Testament.

Wherever Theodore Hardy went… Arras, the mud of Passchendaele, Rossignol Wood, the bridge at Briastre, and finally Rouen… a battered little red book went with him. It was his pocket New Testament, and one can see the bulge of it below the medal ribbons in his studio portrait. It now rests in the Chaplains' Department at Andover.[1]

In it, he marked certain passages and made brief notes. One is struck by how few markings there are, and this must make those passages and words that are marked all the more significant. To handle and read through this little book is to come close to Hardy, to glimpse his inner thoughts, to see what his ministry meant to him, and to feel the source of his inspiration.

Before Hardy's original New Testament was deposited in the Royal Army Chaplain's Museum, the late Canon Michael Westropp of Kirkby Lonsdale painstakingly copied out all the markings in an identical First World War Chaplain's issue New Testament. Bishop George Hacker, late Bishop of Penrith, examined all the markings and very kindly prepared a paper for the author giving his theological interpretation of their meaning and significance.

Passages are marked which would be read to confirmation candidates in shell holes and outposts. The poor soul slowly drowning in the mud at Oosttaverne, the wounded and dying in the dressing stations, a bereaved soldier grieving for a comrade, all would hear words of comfort from this book. One can imagine Hardy drawing consolation and fresh strength in a brief moment of solitude resting in a dug-out before his nocturnal visits to the front line outposts. It is not too fanciful to see him marking a passage by flickering candlelight as he 'listened to the roar, of the guns that hammered Thiepval, Like big breakers on the shore.'[2]

'I speak as to wise men; judge ye what I say' is marked in I Corinthians 10.15. The young men around Hardy had experience of life and death *in extremis* more profound than any previous generation. Most had little education, and before the war probably led a life limited to their own area. Yet they had now seen death, horror, fear, courage and the very highest comradeship as exemplified by Tom Sage VC of the 8th Somersets.

Here then was a true communion of souls with wisdom based not on intellect or age but on common experience and comradeship. Thus, we find...

'for none of us liveth to himself, and no man dieth to himself' (Romans 14.7)

'We are all the children of the light' (Thessalonians 5.5)

'but Christ is all, and in all' (Colossians 4.11)

'And be at peace among yourselves. Now we exhort you, brethren, warn them that are unruly, comfort the feeble minded, support the weak, be patient toward all men' (I Thessalonians 13.14)

'He that spared not his own son, but delivered him up <u>for us all</u>' (Romans 8.32)

For Hardy, there was a natural linkage between the communion of comradeship to the Act of Communion itself. Geoffrey Vallings recalled that

'And Jesus said unto them, I am the bread of life: he that cometh to me shall never hunger; and he that believeth in me shall never thirst' (St. John 6.35). Passage marked by T. B. Hardy in his pocket New Testament. *Photo – Imperial War Museum*

Hardy held 'a fixed idea, that our preparation for confirmation was far too long. Not that he neglected it when opportunity offered, but I have known him present men with what some of my reverend brethren would call no preparation at all. But then we are not all Hardys, and it was the personality of the man which enabled him to do more for a human soul by a few minutes' contact than most of us could do during months of instruction.'[3]

The 'few minutes contact' must have been simple and direct. A series of markings in Matthew's Gospel are almost all at points where Jesus is declared to be 'the Son of God' (often this phrase alone is underlined). It may be that this reflects the current questioning of Jesus's divinity, and is an answer to the common assertion at that time that Jesus was simply a 'good man'.

What Jesus meant to Hardy comes from his annotations in John's Gospel. For Hardy, God was a God of love and mercy, and Jesus was the agent of salvation. The so called 'comfortable words' are marked and underlined: 'For God so loved the world, that he gave his only begotten son, that whosoever believeth in him should not perish, but have everlasting life. For God sent not his Son into the world to condemn the world; but that the world *through him might be saved*' (John 3.16–17).

Then there is John 6.51, 53–58, where Jesus speaks of himself as 'the living bread' and where he promises his presence now and resurrection and eternal life to those who eat this bread. The very ordinary act of receiving Communion takes on a new dimension in the mud and squalor of the trenches when those receiving it are living perpetually under the shadow of death, and these words reinforce that.

We know that Hardy had difficulty with the damnatory clauses in the Athanasian Creed, and his cousin Bessie Hardy remembered: 'A habit of his was: whenever the Psalms for the day were of a vindictive character, he would give a few explanatory notes, before his sermon, showing the difference under the Christian Dispensation. The great truth he always emphasised was God's unlimited love for man.'[4]

In chapter one of Romans, St Paul lists a long catalogue of sins – yet Hardy underlines but one: 'unmerciful'.

With the themes of love and mercy goes reconciliation. The enemy was not to be hated: 'Therefore if thou bring thy gift to the altar, and there rememberest that thy brother hath ought against thee; Leave there thy gift before the altar, and go thy way; first be reconciled to thy brother, and then come and offer thy gift' (Matthew 5.23–24).

There are echoes here of Studdert Kennedy who refused to serve with one officer who kept telling his men that the way to win the war was to kill as many Germans as possible. The Deputy Chaplain General, Bishop Gwynne, recalled how most of the troops defied these instructions and Studdert Kennedy was delighted to hear some Londoners boast that they took more prisoners than any other unit in the British Army.[5]

Maybe this message got through to a sergeant in the 8th Lincolns who stopped Private Jimmy Watson from bayoneting a German with the words, 'Stop, Jim. He's some mother's son.'[6]

'For all the law is fulfilled in one word, even in this; Thou shalt love thy neighbour as thyself' (Galatians 5.14). Whilst in James 1.19 is marked, '… let every man be swift to hear, slow to speak, slow to wrath.'

Aggression and fear were two aspects of psychological stress induced by the war. Shell shock, with men shaking from head to foot and unable to move, was a new and little understood problem. Norman Gladden went through the Flanders campaign and described two such cases: 'A salvo fell venomously across the path ahead of us … A [man] was severely shell shocked; he reeled back towards the sap like one pleasantly tipsy, quite incapable of controlling his reactions.'[7]

Later he describes a regular soldier who had served since 1914: 'A Mons man, a smart soldier and in every way an estimable person … a shell salvo turned him into an incoherent and gesticulating figure. Previous cases that I had seen had been anonymous to me, and although shocking enough in all senses none had had the impact of this incident which involved someone I knew and respected.'[8]

Was Hardy thinking of men such as these when he marked the following passages? 'When the even was come, they brought unto him many that were possessed with devils: and he cast out the spirits with his word, and healed all that were sick' (Matthew 8.16). 'But if I cast out devils by the spirit of God, then the Kingdom of God is come unto you' (Matthew 12.28).

How much Hardy, or anyone else at the time, knew about shell shock it is difficult to say. He was no doubt struggling to understand it and to cope with it and his response was probably instinctive. Yet it is not unreasonable to believe that his quiet, reassuring presence in the aftermath of such an incident did indeed help to salvage men in this condition. Support for this view comes from the leading modern authority on such cases, 'This reasoning is based upon understanding the psychiatric casualty and how such cases should be handled… With every step a soldier takes towards the relative safety of some rearward area the harder it becomes to cure the disability… Men who have received any Christian teaching at their mothers' knees, and even those who have not, do tend to call upon God when afraid in battle.'[9]

By being at the front, Hardy was in the right place to help, and his calm, quiet, familiar strength would give an immediate anchor to such cases.

Even more difficult is the perennial question of how an omnipotent God could allow such a terrible event as the First World War to take place. We know from his sister-in-law's writings that Hardy did not ignore this point. For Hardy, God identified with suffering, and indeed through Christ had suffered Himself.

Mary Hardy tells us that he was fully alive to the fact that life is full of problems which no reason can solve, and mysteries of which we have no explanation. He offered no facile or glib answers to these points. At the heart of it all was a mystery: 'O the depth of the riches both of the wisdom and knowledge of God! how unsearchable are his judgements, and his ways past finding out' (Romans 12.33).

Yet after the long Good Friday was the promise of Easter Day. Death was an ever present reality, part of Hardy's daily round. As Studdert Kennedy wrote: 'All that week I'd buried brothers…'[10]

For Hardy, the promise of eternal life was a reality; Vallings tells us that Hardy, 'Looked upon his wife as alive with him, in constant communion and fellowship. He loved his children intensely, but he believed that he could do no better, if God so willed, than join his beloved wife in the presence of their Lord. Death, as many of us regard it, simply did not exist for him.'[11]

In Revelation 1.17 and 1.18 the three words, '<u>Fear not</u> … <u>death</u>' are underlined.

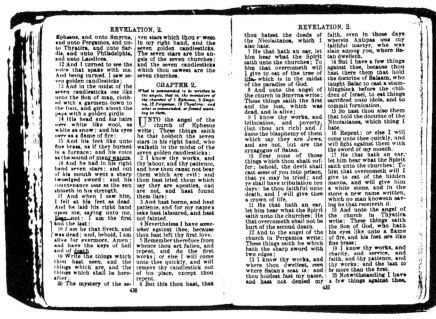

'Fear not … death'

Hardy must have known the Burial Service off by heart by the time he had been in the trenches a few weeks, and no doubt the long passage from I Corinthians 15, which forms the only set reading in the old Prayer Book. We know of his insistence on saying the Burial Service in the incidents at Oosttaverne and Bucquoy. He stood to say the words despite being under enemy fire.

He chose to pick out those verses in which the Easter challenge is presented most forcibly: 'If in this life only we have hope in Christ, we are of all men most miserable. But now is Christ risen from the dead, and become the first fruits of them that slept. For since by man came death, by man came also the resurrection of the dead. For as in Adam all die, even so in Christ shall all be made alive' (I Corinthians 15.19–22).

For those grieving and suffering, and no doubt to himself, he marked two passages in St John (the first with a very rare double mark), 'Ye shall know the truth, and the truth shall make you free' (John 8.32).

And again: 'These things I have spoken unto you, that in me ye might have peace. In the world ye shall have tribulation: but be of good cheer: I have overcome the world' (John 16.33).

BURIAL IN THE TRENCHES

'There are many kinds of sorrow
In this world of Love and Hate,
But there is no sterner sorrow
Than a soldier's for his mate.'

Geoffrey Studdert-Kennedy

'If in this life only we have hope in Christ, we are of all men most miserable. But now is Christ risen from the dead, and become the first fruits of them that slept. For since by man came death, by man came also the resurrection of the dead. For as in Adam all die, even so in Christ shall all be made alive' (I Corinthians 15, 19–22).

We also get glimpses of what Hardy's ministry meant to him. In II Timothy 4.5 he sets himself the challenge: '<u>make full proof of thy ministry</u>'.

Part of that ministry was to go where the vast majority of the Chaplains failed to go: the front line. 'I strived to preach the gospel, not where Christ was named' (Romans 15.20).

In preaching this gospel he spoke of a loving and merciful God, and of the promise of salvation. But we are told that he did not ignore coarse language or behaviour, and behind the diffident shyness was an immensely strong character with a directness of speech when he felt the occasion merited it. The CO of the 8th Somersets tells us, 'His humble nature, his Christ-like personality were most remarkable. As a Minister of God he frequently hit hard; but he was always sympathetic, and while he never compromised with wrong, his addresses to the troops were typical of his natural humility, wherein lay his strength.'[12] This strength through humility, and his natural sympathy for others is seen here, 'Am I therefore become your enemy, because I tell you the truth?' (Galatians 4.16). 'For in that he himself hath suffered being tempted, he is able to succour them that are tempted' (Hebrews 2.18).

Strength through weakness, the paradox at the heart of Christianity, of Christ facing Pilate, had a special message for Hardy as he faced his own inner struggles of life in the trenches.

He has marked a whole string of passages on this theme: 'He said unto me, My grace is sufficient for thee: for my strength is made perfect in weakness … for when I am weak, then am I strong' (II Corinthians 9.10); 'For we are glad when we are weak …' (II Corinthians 13.9); 'Who out of weakness were made strong, waxed valiant in the fight, turned to flight the armies of the aliens' (Hebrews 11.34).

These texts take on a new depth when placed in the context of the daily fatigue, drudgery, discomfort and cold of trench life where everyone, including Hardy, faced the imminent possibility of wounds and death.

His first thought was for others. His faith gave him strength, and his strength must be used for others: 'Who comforteth us in all our tribulations, that we may be able to comfort them which are in any trouble, by the comfort wherewith we ourselves are comforted of God' (II Corinthians 1.4).

'Therefore, my beloved brethren, be ye steadfast, unmoveable, always abounding in the work of the Lord, forasmuch as ye know that your labour is not in vain in the lord' (I Corinthians 15.58).

'Your labour is not in vain in the Lord.' One must wonder if this phrase echoed round and round in Hardy's thoughts during the mind-numbing slog carrying stretchers through the mud of Passchendaele. Amidst all the slaughter and carnage every single life was precious, to be cherished and to be striven for. As exhaustion and fatigue gripped him, and as his elderly body must have shrieked for rest, he was driven on because 'his labour was not in vain in the Lord'. Studdert Kennedy again finds the words in his poem *To Stretcher-Bearers*:

> Stick it, lad, ye'll soon be there now
>
> Want to rest 'ere for a while?
> Let 'im dahn then – gently – gently,
> There ye are, lad. That's the style …
>
> Ow's it goin' now then, sonny?
> 'Ere's that narrow bit o'trench,
> Careful mate, there's some dead Jerries.
>
> Gawd Almighty, what a stench!
> 'Ere we are now, stretcher case, boys,
> Bring him aht a cup o' tea!
>
> IN AS MUCH AS YE HAVE DONE IT
> YE HAVE DONE IT UNTO ME.[13]

To read through Hardy's New Testament and to see his markings is to be taken on a spiritual journey whether one holds the Christian Faith or not. It is to follow in the footsteps of Mr Valiant-for-Truth as he steps out on his own pilgrimage to follow his master. 'Let us therefore come boldly unto the throne of grace, that we may obtain mercy, and find grace to help in time of need' (Hebrews 4.16).

The 'steadfast' theme constantly recurs: 'He <u>steadfastly</u> set his face to go to Jerusalem…' Luke 9.51 (to the death that awaited him on the Cross). There was to be no flinching or turning back: 'Jesus said unto him, No man having put his hand to the plough, and looking back is fit for the Kingdom of God' (Luke 10.62); 'But we are not of them that draw back…' (Hebrews 10.39); 'And let us not be weary in well doing: for in due season we shall reap, if we faint not' (Galatians 6.9).

Perhaps most revealing of all are a clutch of markings in Acts 20 – the only ones to come in the Book of Acts, which must make them all the more significant. Here in Paul's speech to the Elders at Ephesus, as he stopped off on his journey to Jerusalem with all its forecasts of imprisonment and possible death, we catch a glimpse of Hardy's inspiration: 'He hasted, if it were possible for him, to be at Jerusalem the day of Pentecost … Serving the Lord with all humility of mind, and with many tears, and temptations, which befell me … Testifying, repentance toward God, and faith to our Lord Jesus Christ … But none of these things move me, neither count I my life dear unto myself, so that I might finish my course <u>with</u> joy, and the ministry, which I have received of the Lord Jesus, to testify the gospel of the grace of God' (Acts 20.16, 19, 21, 24).

The last of Hardy's markings – and there are only four of them – appear at the end in the Book of Revelation. Two we have mentioned, 'Fear not … Death'

The last two, he must have seen as the Lord's word to him in his prayers – a command to go through into the unknown; confirmation that his

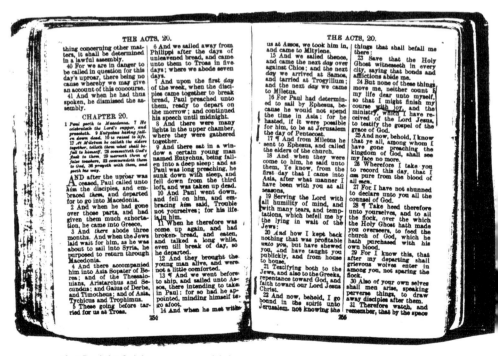

… so that I might finish my course with joy …

desperately sacrificial ministry was right; and commendation in just those words which his humble and unassuming nature would delight to accept, 'I know thy works: behold, I have set before thee an open door, and no man can shut it; for thou hast a little strength, and hast kept my word, and hast not denied my name' (Revelation 3.8).

The last words come almost as a shout of triumph overwhelming the tumult and misery of war, and his own last journey on that plank bridge over the River Selle. 'And I heard as it were the voice of a great multitude, and as the voice of many waters, and as the voice of mighty thunderings, saying, Alleluia: for the Lord God omnipotent reigneth' (Revelation 19.6).

I was especially grateful to Miss Patricia Hastings Hardy for allowing me to see her Grandfather's New Testament before she deposited it with the Chaplains' Department for safe keeping. I was also very grateful to Canon Michael Westropp for carefully and laboriously copying out Theodore Hardy's markings and annotations into an identical copy of the New Testament. I am much indebted to the Bishop of Penrith for helping me to interpret the various passages, and for his very considerable help in other ways.

Appendix: The Rt Revd George Hacker's notes on the annotations in Hardy's New Testament

Author's note: I am very grateful to The Rt Revd Bishop George Hacker, former Bishop of Penrith, for providing this appendix to chapter twelve, the full version of his notes on the annotations made by Theodore Bayley Hardy in his pocket New Testament.

The first thing that strikes one is how few markings there are – some in almost every book, but surprisingly few, and those often not the obvious ones. This must make those passages and words that are marked all the more significant.

Apart from Matthew and Mark, the markings are mainly of two kinds – a line in the margin marking a verse or part of a verse; a line underlining a word or phrase. It is very rare for more than one verse to be marked, though some of the markings occur in 'clumps', drawing attention to particular verses in a single passage.

Matthew and Mark have a series of numbers in the margin. It looks as if Hardy went through these two Gospels and noted all the miracles that our Lord performed. In Matthew these are interspersed by small letters which seem to be drawing attention to different groups' reactions – Scribes, Pharisees, Disciples of John etc. There are also some capitals in both Gospels which seem to have to do with the Authorities' opposition to Jesus and the steps which led to his death. What the purpose of these are is not at all obvious. However, the underlinings in Matthew's Gospel are almost all at points where Jesus is declared to be 'the Son of God' (often this phrase alone is underlined), and it could be that this reflects the current questioning of Jesus's divinity – Hardy's own research so that he would have an answer to the ordinary man's estimate of Jesus as simply a 'good man'. Further on he has marked Colossians 4.6 'Let your speech be always with grace, seasoned with salt, that ye may know how ye <u>ought to answer</u> every man' (Cf. I Peter 3.15). And of course it could have been for his own benefit too. We know that he had difficulties over the 'damnation' clauses in the Athanasian Creed. He would have been less than human if he had not had to face questionings and doubts at some time. There is a double mark (very rare) by John 8.32: 'Ye shall know the truth'; but it cannot have been a major matter – most of the markings assume a simple and humble trust: 'These things I have spoken unto you, that in me ye might have peace. In the world ye shall have tribulation: but be of good cheer: I have overcome the world.' (John 16.33).

To follow Hardy's markings in his pocket New Testament is to be taken on a spiritual pilgrimage. Certain themes recur again and again. 'Steadfastly' is underlined in Luke 9.51, 'He <u>steadfastly</u> set his face to go to Jerusalem' (to the death that awaited him on the Cross), and that must have been how it must always have felt to Hardy on his way up to the Front. 'But we are not of them that draw back...' he has marked in Hebrews 10.39, and underlined '<u>if we faint not</u>' in Galatians 6.9 and '<u>fear not</u>' and '<u>death</u>' in Revelation 1.17,18. 'No man, having put his hand to the plough, and looking back, is fit for the kingdom of God' (Luke 9.62).

We can see too where he drew his strength from. 'For in that he himself hath suffered being tempted, he is able to succour them that are tempted' (Hebrews 2.18). Both the Lord's time of temptation in the wilderness and his agony in the Garden of Gethsemane are marked at points where angels ministered and strengthened him, and we can easily see how these particular times in our Lord's ministry would have a special message for Hardy in his own inner struggles, as again and again he had to face the very real possibility of wounds and death. There are also a whole string of verses picked out on the theme of strength in weakness: 'He said unto me, My grace is sufficient for thee: for my strength is made perfect in weakness ... for when I am weak, then am I strong' (II Corinthians 12.9, 10); 'For we are glad when we are weak ...' (II Corinthians 13.9); 'For God hath not given us the spirit of fear; but of power, and of love, and of a sound mind' (II Timothy 1.7); 'Who out of weakness were made strong, waxed valiant in fight, turned to flight the armies of the aliens' (Hebrews 11.34). Very familiar texts all of these, but they take on a new depth and seriousness when viewed against the background of weariness, drudgery, cold, fear and death, which made up daily life in the trenches.

There are also some precious glimpses into what his ministry meant to him. 'That we may be able to comfort them which are in any trouble, by the comfort wherewith we ourselves are comforted of God' (II Corinthians 1.4) is a very revealing passage, as is Galatians 1.10, 'For if I yet pleased men, I should not be the servant of Christ'. As we know, Hardy refused to follow the 'sensible' way of the majority of Chaplains preaching and ministering to the crowds that thronged the base camps and depots. His way was simply to be with the men where they needed him most – in the front line, and sometimes beyond it in no-man's-land itself. So Romans 11.33, 'I am the Apostle of the Gentiles', is a particularly significant marking (and 'Gentiles' is underlined twice more in a later chapter). Clearly he saw himself as having a ministry to those whom most padres scarcely touched – 'I strived to preach the gospel, not where Christ was named' (Romans 15.20) – and his willingness to be with the men, wherever and whoever they were, ensured that this was in fact how it worked out. Perhaps most revealing of all are a clutch of markings in Acts 20 – the only ones in the whole of the Book of Acts, which must make them all the more significant. Here in Paul's speech to the Elders at Ephesus as he stopped off on his journey to Jerusalem with all its forecasts of imprisonment and possible death, we catch more than a glimpse of what inspired this very ordinary yet remarkable man:

He hasted, if it were possible for him, to be at Jerusalem the day of Pentecost ... Serving the Lord with all humility of mind, and with many tears, and temptations, which befell me by the lying in wait of the Jews ... Testifying, repentance toward God, and faith toward our Lord

Jesus Christ. But none of these things move me, neither count I my life dear unto myself, so that I might finish my course with joy, and the ministry, which I have received of the Lord Jesus, to testify the gospel of the grace of God. (Acts 20.16, 19, 21, 24).

When we come to that Gospel itself and what he actually said to the men and what he preached about, we are on less certain ground. Perhaps the longer marked passages give a clue here – certainly they are all of a piece with what the other markings show about him. John 3.15, 16, 19, the 'Comfortable Words', 'God so loved the world, that he gave his only begotten Son …', with '<u>through him might be saved</u>' underlined, and verse 19, which sees judgment as a rejection of the light picked out, are a reflection perhaps of his own theological position and earlier difficulties with the Athanasian Creed. Then there is John 6.51, 53–58, where Jesus speaks of himself as 'the living bread' and where he promises his presence now and resurrection and eternal life to those who eat this bread. Again the very ordinary act of receiving Communion takes on a new dimension in the mud and squalor of the trenches, when those receiving it are living perpetually under the shadow of death, and these words reinforce that. Of particular significance is I Corinthians 15.19–22. Hardy must have known the Burial Service off by heart by the time he had been in the trenches a few weeks and no doubt all of the long passage from I Corinthians 15, which forms the only set reading in the old Prayer Book. But he has chosen to pick out these verses in which the Easter challenge is presented most forcibly: 'If in this life only we have hope in Christ, we are of all men most miserable. But now is Christ risen from the dead, and become the first-fruits of them that slept …' (I Corinthians 15.19, 20). In the previous chapter Hardy has underlined: 'If the trumpet give an <u>uncertain sound</u>, who shall prepare himself to the battle' (I Corinthians 14.8). There is no uncertainty here.

Finally, of all the markings, the one which stood out for me was one of the last that I came to – Revelation 3.8. I felt with this that I had somehow got inside the man, and got inside him at his prayers. For this must surely have come as the Lord's word to him – command to go through into the unknown; confirmation that his desperately sacrificial ministry was right; and commendation in just those words which his humble and unassuming nature would delight to accept. 'I know thy works: behold, I have set before thee an open door, and no man can shut it: for thou hast a little strength, and hast kept my word, and hast not denied my name' (Revelation 3.8).

Footnote: Bishop George used these notes as the basis of a sermon he preached in the Colours to the Chapel Service at the Royal Military Academy, Sandhurst on 6th August, 1995.

Chapter Thirteen

Mr Valiant-For-Truth Crosses the River

'So he passed over, and all the trumpets sounded for him on the other side.'
Pilgrim's Progress, John Bunyan

Throughout the spring and early summer of 1918 the Germans continued their effort for a decisive breakthrough. They drove deeply into British and French territory, recapturing all the area in Flanders so dearly won by the British the previous autumn. But the decisive victory never came, and in the process of attempting it the Germans exhausted themselves.

During this period the Lincolns and Somersets carried out a continual round of trench duty in the Bucquoy sector. Whenever they withdrew for a few days rest, the padre would stay in the line with the relieving battalion (usually the 4th Middlesex, the 13th Rifle Brigade, the 2nd Canterbury (New Zealand), or the 5th King's Own Yorkshire Light Infantry). The usual pattern would be six days in the trenches, six days on working parties behind the line, and, if they were lucky, six days to rest and clean up equipment.

The final German effort came in mid-July to the East of Reims, but its success was minimal. The Germans had clearly shot their bolt, and by now the Allies were being re-enforced by 300,000 American troops a month. The tide was about to turn. The 8th of August (the day before Hardy received his VC) was described by Ludendorff as 'Black Tuesday' when the British, Australians and Canadians advanced in the Somme.

'August 8th was the black day of the German Army in the history of the war… It put the decline of our fighting power beyond all doubt … The war must be ended.' Three months and three days later it was.

When the 8th Somersets gathered in the barn at Souastre to greet and cheer their highly embarrassed chaplain, for many it was to be the last time they would be together. With the 8th Lincolns they immediately moved into support positions ready to take part in the final offensive.

At 4.50 am on 21 August, the whistles blew and they climbed out of the trenches in heavy mist to attack Bucquoy. As usual a now much decorated non-combatant went with them.

Five days of fierce fighting followed, during which they advanced over six miles and captured Bapaume. The Lincolns suffered 177 casualties and the

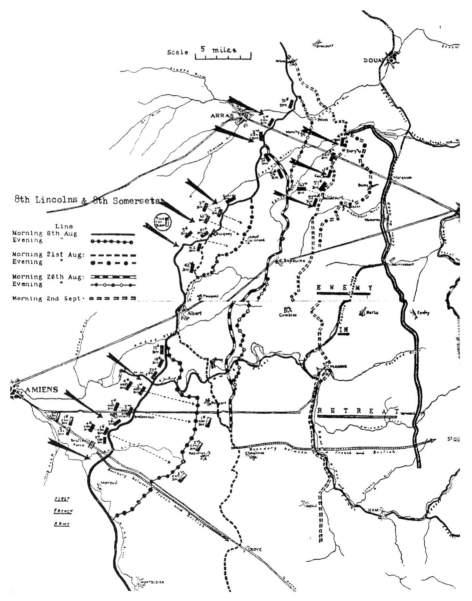

Opening of the Final British Offensive. 8th August–9th September, 1918.

Somersets 170. Colonel Hardyman went forward in a tank to reconnoitre the ground. He was killed by a shell when he got out of the tank for a better view. Hardy's friend Captain Madden was awarded the Military Cross, and Company Sergeant Major Yaw the Distinguished Conduct Medal.

The advance continued as other brigades leapfrogged through, allowing the two battalions of Lincolns and Somersets to rest and recover at Achiet. It was whilst they were there that a new honour was conferred on Hardy. He was appointed a Chaplain to the King, an honour within the King's personal gift.

Lieutenant Colonel Sheringham, the new CO of the 8th Somersets remembered the occasion. 'The news came that His Majesty the King desired the Padre to become one of his Chaplains in Ordinary. I remember so well his coming to me and shyly producing the letter from the Lord Chamberlain. The Regimental band was playing at the time; we were in rest billets for three days before again taking up the advance. There was a large throng of men gathered to hear the band. I collared the Padre, and took him along to where the band was playing, and, when the piece was finished, I announced to those present I had something to tell them. I told them I had

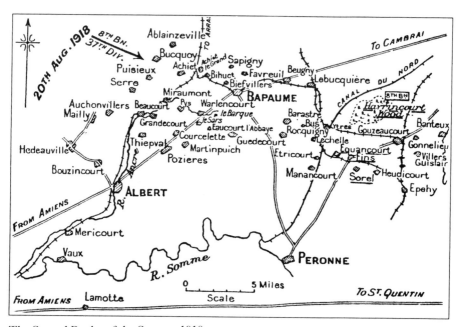

The Second Battles of the Somme, 1918.

found the Padre out, and then read out to them the letter from the Lord Chamberlain. Such a cheer went up as I shall always remember.

'The Padre was then called upon for a speech, and I shall never forget how he belittled his own doings – said that whilst he felt the honour of the favour which His Majesty had conferred on him, he felt that the honour was really conferred on the battalion, *not* on him. He was only afraid lest it might mean that he would be obliged to go home and leave his friends in the two battalions, if he accepted. He said that his greatest happiness in life was to be among his friends in the two battalions.'[1]

Hardy's comment that he might be obliged to go home hints at the pressure being put on him to do so. The King had been profoundly impressed by Hardy's record when he met him, and together with the Bishop of Carlisle. was the moving force behind an attempt to save him from further risk. The Bishop offered him the vacant living of Caldbeck (John Peel country in the Northern Lakeland Fells) at twice the income of Hutton Roof, but Hardy would not accept. The matter is recorded in the *Carlisle Diocesan Gazette*: 'The Bishop offered him the vacant rectory of Caldbeck, which, although most attractive to him by reason of his country tastes, love of natural beauty, fondness of country folk, delight in walking and climbing, he self-denyingly declined on the ground that as he had been absent from his little parish of

Warrant Officers and Sergeants of the 8th Battalion, the Lincolnshire Regiment, at Frasnes-le-Gosselies in January 1919, prior to demobilization.

Hutton Roof so long without any murmur from the parishioners, he felt it was his duty to return and serve them when the war was over.'[2]

His friend and colleague Geoffrey Vallings tried to get him to change his mind, but Hardy deflected him with a self-mocking comment. 'He hoped for his Majesty's sake that one of his duties as Honorary Chaplain would not be to preach for him.'[3]

The campaign continued, this time with Colonel Hitch, CO of the 8th Lincolns trying to influence him. 'I had a long talk with him as to the advisability of him accepting some post at the Base, a matter which I had talked over previously with the Divisional and Corps Chaplains, and which we were agreed was what ought to happen. He had done his bit we said, and now it was time for him to leave us for an easier life at the Base, where he could carry on his work backed by the enormous prestige his decorations had won him. Well, the Padre came back, and we started to talk about this work at the Base, but it was recognised from the start that my arguments would be useless, and I must admit that I was immensely pleased and proud to think that they were so. However, I stuck to it for some time, and finally I compromised and agreed to let the matter drop until the next time we came out of the line for a rest – but the occasion never came, for the next time we went into action was our advance up to the River Selle.'[4]

It should have come as no surprise that Hardy would not be moved. Two years of comradeship bound him to the men of the two battalions. Witness after witness speaks of his reluctance to leave the line. That was where he was happiest and that was where he was going to stay. Colonel Hitch remembered trying to find him. 'It was eleven o'clock at night and the Confirmation was to take place the next day at midday at the village about eight miles back; but the Padre could nowhere be found. He was doing his round of posts, and it was only at four o'clock in the morning that we found him and packed him off to rear quarters. This was one of the many occasions when he went something like forty-eight hours without sleep. I have often wondered whether he managed to get a shave before meeting the Bishop, as he left us with four-days' growth.'[5]

Geoffrey Vallings remembered him collecting confirmation candidates. 'He literally pulled men out of the shell-hole line, going from one to the other, collecting them and walking down with them. Dead-beat, spent and weary, he arrived with that extraordinarily beautiful smile on his face, a veritable triumph of the spiritual over the physical.'[6]

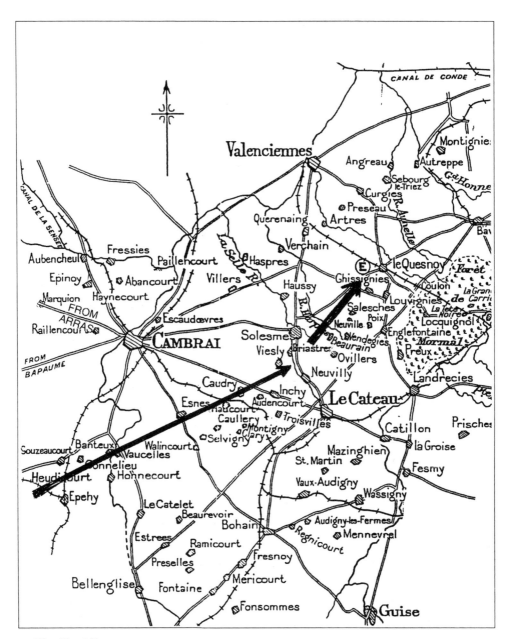

The Final Days
Map taken from The History of the Lincolnshire Regiment, 1914–1919.
Line of advance by the 8th Lincolns and 8th Somersets in October, 1918. Theodore Hardy
was wounded crossing the River Selle at Briastres in the early hours of 11th October. The
two Battalions saw only eight more days of action, and had reached point 'E' when the
Armistice came into force on 11th November.

The Bishop of Carlisle, no doubt prodded by the King, tried yet again. He wrote and asked Hardy to reconsider the offer of the living at Caldbeck. But Hardy would not shift. The most he would promise was to think the matter over and to consult Elizabeth. His reply to the Bishop ends, '... but perhaps I shall be called away soon, and there will be no need to make a decision.'[7]

And so it proved to be.

On 4 September, the Lincolns and the Somersets joined the advance again. By this time the days of trench warfare were gone. A war of movement had at last resumed. The Germans slowly retreated, but as the British followed them they were met with heavy machine-gun fire and artillery shelling. By the time they were relieved on 11 September, the two battalions had advanced another six miles to Havrincourt Wood but both had lost over 100 casualties. Yet they all felt that the end of the war was in sight, for the Germans were now in headlong retreat back towards their own frontier.

In the days that followed, both battalions gave support to the advance troops as they went forward across the old Somme battlefields. The *History of the Somerset Light Infantry* gives a graphic description

Private Jim Watson of the 8th Lincolns. Private Watson volunteered soon after his 18th birthday in 1915. He served with the 8th Lincolns throughout Theodore Hardy's time with the battalion. He was in the team of Lewis Gunners and stretcher bearers crossing the River Selle when Hardy received his fatal wound. Jim Watson remembers Hardy saying, 'I've been hit. I'm sorry to be a nuisance.' Private Watson lived in Grantham, his home town for many years and remembered buying sweets from the future Mrs. Thatcher in her father's shop.

of what they saw: 'The utter desolation of the Somme country at this period was terrible to see. Gaping shell holes were everywhere, roads had been almost blotted out and had become mere tracks: villages that had once been the habitations of men no longer existed as such, tumbled masses of bricks and stones and rubbish marking the sites ... The holocausts of 1917 and 1918... had left this country bare and barren, a noisome place, the earth blood soaked and stinking with the rotting corpses which lay beneath its troubled surface. Everywhere traces of the beaten and defeated enemy were seen from the broken gun carriages, transport wagons, equipment and other abandoned war material, with the dead still crying silently for burial.'[8]

On 8 October it was the turn of the Lincolns and Somersets to take on the brunt of the fighting yet again, for the Germans were still putting up fierce resistance in a fighting retreat. Their task was to attack to the east of Cambrai towards the River Selle; their stint was to last four days, and they still faced a determined enemy. 'In spite of heavy machine-gun and artillery fire the advance went on … machine-gunners raked the line of Somerset men. In the latter stages of the War the enemy's machine-gunners were the bravest troops in the German Army. With extraordinary tenacity they clung to every position … They were brave fellows those German machine-gunners: they fought with their backs against the wall.'[9]

By nightfall on 10 October, the two battalions which had fought alongside each other for over three years, were near the banks of the River Selle. 'When darkness had fallen all Companies sent out patrols to report any available crossings over the River Selle. They returned with the information that no crossings could be found, that the Selle was from twenty to thirty feet wide, and that there were no trees which could be felled for the construction of temporary bridges. But about 3.00 am on the 11th an officer of the 153rd Company, RE, said that he would endeavour to erect some sort of bridge. B and C Companies of the 8th Somersets and one company of the Lincolns were then instructed… to cross the river if ordered to do so. Soon the battalion had established its front on the eastern banks of the Selle, with the Somersets on the left and the Lincolns on the right.'[10]

In the darkness, a small figure looked across to the other side. He crossed the river to his friends. 'It's only me, boys' he said. After a while he told them he would have to go. Minutes later they heard the machine gun open fire. They never saw him again, but he would stay with them always.

Note the motor ambulance heading west and the horse artillery moving east towards the front. Here Theodore Bayley Hardy received his fatal wound.

Theodore Hardy had been shot through the thigh, and at first it was hoped that his wound would not be too serious. His fellow stretcher bearers braved a hail of machine-gun bullets coming across the river to get him back to a dressing station.

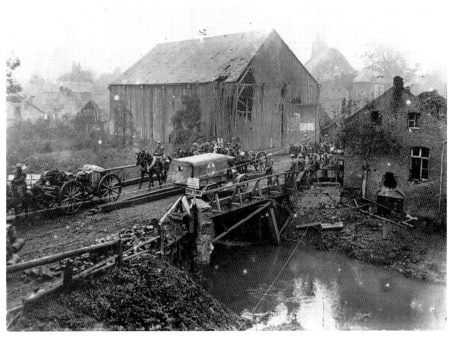

The bridge over the River Selle, 28 October 1918.

Private Maurice Calvert was there. 'He said to the stretcher bearers, in a voice husky with weakness and pain, "I'm sorry to give you all this trouble boys, when you are urgently needed elsewhere". His last thought as he was carried away was not for himself, you see.'[11]

Blood transfusion and intravenous fluid replacements were barely considered or made available to the medical authorities in the First World War. Many died from shock and loss of blood. Hardy was no exception, and the years of physical punishment and exhaustion had weakened him.

He was evacuated by train, in itself an ordeal, over 100 miles to the No. 2 Red Cross Hospital at Rouen. Elizabeth was sent for. Douglas Carey, the Assistant Chaplain General, saw him there. 'I saw him for a few moments… Pneumonia had not yet set in, but he was very tired from his journey and not wholly conscious. He mistook me at first for his son, and called me by his pet name for his boy, who, he thought, might have turned up to see him.'[12]

Theodore Bayley Hardy VC DSO MC died a week after being wounded on 18 October 1918. Three weeks later the war was over.

Douglas Carey, whom Theodore Hardy had badgered to be allowed to go up to the front, conducted the Funeral Service. Elizabeth was able to be present. Six chaplains acted as bearers. His old friend from the Kirkby Lonsdale Scout troop, Jonty Wilson, managed to be there.

Back at the front, Colonel Sheringham had to break the news to the 8th Somersets. 'I shall never forget the expression of the men when the news came that the Padre was dead. There was an atmosphere of deep emotion. We all felt, I know, that we had all lost a very dear personal friend. Very few eyes were dry. This can easily be understood when one remembers that Padre Hardy was in very truth a brother to all those young soldiers who now heard the news of his death. These lads were, like us all, very proud of him.'[13]

Colonel Hitch of the 8th Lincolns wrote to Mary Hardy. 'It was a tremendous shock when we heard that he had died. We had a short memorial service, and it was the most moving and sincere service I have ever attended … The service was voluntary, and officers and men of nearly all the units with whom he had come into contact were there, though there was, of course, a majority of our men. What his loss has meant to us is more than I can express, but his name will always be recalled with reverence, and to those of us who knew him really intimately, a great blank has appeared in our daily lives.'[14]

Only a Comrade

Only a comrade is dead,
But relieved, thank God, from pain,
'Ere he soared in flight
Far beyond our sight,
Where heroic spirits reign.

Only a Padre, and old
With an unassuming grace.
In his heart of gold
Was true courage bold,
And love-light shone in his face.

Only a pal of my own
On the road we twain have trod,

Till he passed alone
Through the great unknown
To shew me the way to God.

Only one man, just one more
In the roll of England's fame,
Yet his friends of yore
And the cross he wore
Are honoured by this man's name.

The Reverend G.R. Vallings DSO SCF

The original handwritten version of the poem was in the possession of Miss Patricia Hastings Hardy and is now in the Royal Army Chaplain's Department Museum. The poem was published in *The Golden Horse*

Shoe, the journal of the 37th Division, with a few minor differences to the original. A copy of the magazine is in the Somerset County Record Office, Taunton.

Tree in Rossignol Wood. Poppies left by Hutton Roof villagers and Hardy's granddaughter

Memorial to Reverend Theodore Bayley Hardy VC DSO MC, St John's Church, Hutton Roof.

Grave 7, Row J, Plot V, Block S. St. Sever Military Cemetery, Rouen.

Memorial plaque, Carlisle Cathedral.

Hutton Roof War Memorial in St John's churchyard.

In 1919, Colonel Hitch wrote to the authorities of Westminster Abbey suggesting a memorial to Hardy be placed on the Abbey. So far this has not happened.

The parishioners of Hutton Roof and Lupton prepared an illuminated address, and collected funds to buy a gold watch, both to be presented to their vicar when he returned after the war. Sadly this never occurred and the illuminated address now hangs on the wall of St John the Divine Church in Hutton Roof.[15]

The author

DAVID RAW was educated at Bradford Grammar School, and London University where he graduated in History and Education. He was a head teacher in Cumbria before his retirement.

He is the author of *The Bradford Pals* (Pen & Sword, 2006) and recently completed a Masters degree in First World War Studies at the University of Wolverhampton. He now lives in Scotland and is currently working on the diaries of Major General Granville Egerton, commander of the 52nd Lowland Division in Gallipoli. He occasionally leads tours of the Western Front.

His interest in T.B. Hardy began when he first saw the memorial tablet in Carlisle Cathedral in 1988 when leading a school visit.

Notes

Chapter 1
1. 1861 and 1871 Census.
2. The Royal Commercial Traveller Schools (author, Ronald Edwards).
3. George Hardy, death certificate, 13 October 1870.
4. Devon Record Office 3992F.
5. Werner E.E. (1986) 'Resilient offspring of alcoholics, A longitudinal study from birth to age 18'. *Journal of studies on alcohol* 47 (1) pp.34–40.
6. 1871 Census.
7. Admission book, Royal Commercial Travellers School, London Metropolitan Archives, Acc/0992.
8. Edwards, op. cit.
9. 1881 Census.
10. Mary Hardy, *Hardy VC, An appreciation*, (Skeffington, London 1920)
11. Royal Commercial Travellers School, London Metropolitan Archives, Acc/0992.
12. 1881 census.
13. City of London School Archives, kindly supplied by Terry Heard, school archivist.
14. History of City of London School, A.E. Douglas Smith (1965).
15. Speech by Rt Hon H.H. Asquith MP at City of London School John Carpenter Society reunion 1895.
16. Douglas Smith op. cit.
17. School magazine, City of London School archives, courtesy Terry Heard.
18. Douglas Smith op. cit.
19. H.W. Nevinson, *Last Changes, Last Chances,* Nisbet & Co. Ltd (1928).
20. C.E. Montague, Disenchantment, p.70, Chatto & Windus, (1922).
21. Douglas Smith, op cit. Dr. Edwin Abbott's book *Flatlands* is still in print and regarded as an all-time philosophical classic.
22. Douglas Smith, ibid.
23. Mary Hardy, op. cit.
24. University of London archives, register of graduates.
25. Mary Hardy, op. cit.
26. Ibid.
27. I am grateful to Jim Davison of the Great Victoria Street Baptist Meeting House, Belfast for the photograph of the church and a copy of the Hardys' Marriage Certificate.

Chapter 2
1. The City of London School moved to a new site in Cheapside in the City in 1834, and moved again as it expanded to Victoria Embankment in 1883. The School had, and still has, strong musical traditions with a link with the Choir of the Chapel Royal. It was administered by the City Corporation.
2. Nottingham High School archives (NHSA).

3. NHSA.
4. NHSA.
5. NHSA.
6. NHSA.
7. 1901 Census.
8. NHSA.
9. Mary Hardy, op cit.
10. Ibid.
11. NHSA.
12. *Nottingham Guardian Journal*, 25 September 1965.
13. Keith Sagar, *The Life of D.H. Lawrence*, p.23, (Eyre Methuen, London, 1980).
14. NHSA.
15. Chaz Bowyer, *Albert Ball VC*, (Bridge Books, 1977).

Chapter 3
1. Hardy, op.cit.
2. Laura Ridding, *George Ridding, schoolmaster and bishop: Forty-third head master of Winchester, 1866–1884, first bishop of Southwell, 1884–1904*. University of Michigan press, 1908.
3. The Thoroton Society website, Nottingham.
4. Neville Benyon, 'Bishop Gwynne: Deputy Chaplain-General to the British Armies on the Western Front during the First World War' (*Wolverhampton Military Studies*), 2016.
5. *History of Burton Joyce*. Local publication.
6. St. Helen's Church Register, Burton Joyce, 31 May 1899.

Chapter 4
1. James Bibby, *A History of Bentham*, 1931. Much of the information in this section is derived from *The History of Bentham Grammar School, 1726–1976*, Huddleston, Wilson and Warbrick, 1976. Published by Titus Wilson of Kendal.
2. The living of Hutton Roof was in the gift of the Vicar of Kirkby Lonsdale. It provided an income of £165 per annum. The parish had a population of 245 in the 1901 census. There was a school, and also a small Methodist chapel. The church (dedicated to St. John) had been rebuilt in 1880. The small neighbouring parish of Lupton was included in Hardy's care.
3. Mary Hardy, op. cit.
4. Ibid.
5. Ibid.
6. Jonty Wilson, Notes for Remembrance Sunday, in possession of his daughter, Mrs. Cox. Jonty Wilson was the subject of a biography *A Cumbrian Blacksmith* published by Dalesman Books in 1978.
7. Letters in possession of Miss Patricia Hastings Hardy and now deposited with the Royal Army Chaplains' Department, Andover.
8. *London Gazette*, 23 July 1909 and 11 November 1915.

Chapter 5
1. See Norman Gladden, *Ypres* 1977 pp. 26–27, Kimber 1967. Also William Allison and John Fairley, *The Monocled Mutineer*, Quartet Books, 1979.
2. *Wilfred Owen: Collected Letters* pp. 67–68, edited by H. Owen and J. Bell, London 1967.
3. Letter from Rev D.F. Carey to Mrs Mary Hardy, quoted in *Hardy VC* Skeffington, 1919. Rev Douglas Falkland Carey (1874–1947) was Assistant Chaplain General on the Western Front, later Chaplain to Sandhurst College, and then Dean of Guernsey.

4. Alan Lloyd, *The War in the Trenches* pp. 133–139, (Hart-Davis MacGibbon, 1976).
5. Siegfried Sasson, *Memoirs of an Infantry Officer*, (Faber and Faber, 1965).
6. C.E. Montague, *Disenchantment*. op. cit.
7. Private information to the author.
8. Quoted in Lloyd, op. cit.
9. Lloyd, op. cit.
10. Bernard Martin, *Poor Bloody Infantry, A Subaltern on the Western Front, 1916–17*, (John Murray, 1987).

Chapter 6

1. William Purcell, *Woodbine Willie – a study of Geoffrey Studdert Kennedy*, p.15, (Mowbray 1962).
2. Ibid. p.11.
3. Mary Hardy, *Hardy V.C.* op. cit. Letter written by Geoffrey Studdert Kennedy, pp. 24–27.
4. Letter written by T.B. Hardy to Rev. D.F. Carey, 24.7.1918.
5. Mary Hardy, op. cit. p.23.

Chapter 7

1. *Hardy, VC*, op cit.
2. Map from J. Reynolds, Allen L. Churchill, Francis Trevelyan Miller (eds.): *The Story of the Great War*, Volume V. New York.
3. Marvin Swartz, *The Union of Democratic Control in British politics during the First World War*, (Clarendon), 1971.
4. *A Challenge*, poems by John Hay Maitland Hardyman DSO MC, foreword by Norman Hugh Romanes, 1920.
5. Morel Papers, London School of Economics.
6. Imperial War Museum Sound archive, Lieutenant Cecil Tubbs.
7. Martin Middlebrook, *First Day of the Somme*, Allen Lane, 1971.
8. Colonel Repington, *The First World War, 1914–18*, Constable, 1920.
9. Haig Diary, 9 February 1917.
10. Casualty Figures obtained from Simpson, *The History of the Lincolnshire Regiment, 1914–18,* Medici Society, 1931. Middlebrook, himself a Lincolnshire man, quotes the difficulties facing a stretcher bearer in the 8th Lincolns (Sgt. A.P. Britton) on the first day of the Somme: 'As we had no stretchers we had to use sheets of corrugated iron and by the end of the day we had all cut our fingers.' *The First Day of the Somme*, p.228.
11. *The Wipers Times*, a trench newspaper.
12. Martin, op. cit. pp.47/48.
13. *The Sunday Times*, 9 November 1958.
14. Interview with author, 10 August 1986.
15. Mary Hardy, op. cit. Lieutenant Captain Madden was to receive a bar to his MC during the German attack in which Theodore Hardy received his fatal wound. By this time he was a company commander in the 8th Somersets.
16. Ibid. Vallings to Mary Hardy.
17. Ibid.
18. Ibid.
19. Ibid.
20. Letter 22 March 1917. With Miss Patricia Hastings Hardy. Now at Royal Army Chaplains' Department.
21. *8th (S.) BATT LINCOLNSHIRE REGIMENT*, compiled by Lieutenant Arthur Tyler Hitch DSO, commanding officer of the 8th Lincolnshire Regiment.

22. Captain J.C. Dunn DSO MC *The War the Infantry Knew* , Bright, London, 1938. p 485.
23. Ibid. p.487.
24. Ibid. p.555–6.
25. Letter in *The Times*, 27 May 1939.
26. Dunn, op cit pp. 491–2.
27. Ibid p. 492.

Chapter 8
1. Letter from Reverend Geoffrey Vallings DSO (senior chaplain to 37th Division) to Mrs Mary Hardy, 1919.
2. General Edmund Allenby, Order of the Day issued 12 April 1917 to 3rd Army units.
3. Eyewitness account. Private in 1st Gordon Highlanders, quoted in Lloyd, *opus cit*. p.151.
4. Hardy, op cit. Vallings, letter.

Chapter 9
1. Haig, Despatch to War Cabinet, 12 June 1917.
2. Interview with author, 10 August 1986.
3. Wyrall, *History of the Somerset Light Infantry, 1914–1919*, Methuen, 1927. pp.194–7.
4. Ibid.
5. Ibid.
6. Captain H.O. Pring MC, letter to Mary Hardy, 1919, *op. cit.*
7. Lt Col C.J. de B. Sheringham DSO MC, letter to Mary Hardy, 1919. Sheringham was a staff captain (13th Rifle Brigade) and later CO 8th Somersets.
8. Lt Col Challener CB CMG DSO, commander 63rd Infantry Brigade, letter to Mary Hardy, 1919.
9. Citation for DSO, *London Gazette*, 7 March 1918.
10. Vallings, ibid.
11. General Hubert Gough, *The Fifth Army*, (Hodder & Stoughton, 193)1, p.205.
12. Colonel Repington, *The First World War, 1914–1918*, Vol. II, pp.30–1. Constable, 1920.
13. Vallings, ibid.
14. Ibid.
15. B.H. Liddell Hart, *History of the First World War* (Cassell & Co, 1930.
16. Lt Col. A.T. Hitch DSO, letter to Mary Hardy, 1919, ibid.
17. Challener, ibid.
18. Sheringham, ibid. Also Letter from Private Maurice Calvert to his father: 'When one Battalion relieves another in the line, the out-going officer hands the Padre over to the incoming officer as "trench stores"; that is, a permanent trench fixture.' Mary Hardy, ibid.
19. Sergeant Major R. Yaw DCM, Letter to Mary Hardy, 1919, ibid.
20. Watson, ibid.
21. Hitch, ibid.

Chapter 11
1. War Diary, 8th Battalion, Lincolnshire Regiment. In the February 1918 reorganisation, many brigades were reduced to three battalions. Thus the 10th Yorks & Lancs left 63rd Brigade.
2. op. cit.
3. *London Gazette*, 11 July 1918, citation for VC.
4. Letter to Mary Hardy, 1919.

5. Letter to Mary Hardy, 1919
6. Letter to Mary Hardy, 1919.
7. Ibid.
8. Elizabeth Hardy, letter to William Hastings Hardy, August 1918.
9. IWM, sound archive.
10. Information from Patricia Hardy.
11. Letter to Archdeacon I.D. Neill from Mrs. Joy Mott, 20 September 1965.
12. IWM Sound archive.
13. Letter to Mary Hardy from Bishop Gwynne.
14. History of the Somerset Light Infantry. Details of Hardyman's award and death on pp.
    307/309.
15. IWM sound archive. German offensive in July.

Chapter 12

1. The New Testament was presented to the Chaplain's Department on permanent loan by
    Miss Patricia Hastings Hardy in April 1988.
2. G.G.A. Studdert Kennedy, 'His Mate' in *The Unutterable Beauty*, 1927, Mowbray.
3. Vallings in Mary Hardy, opus cit.
4. Hardy, ibid.
5. H.C. Jackson, *Pastor of the Nile, A life of Bishop L.H. Gwynne, Deputy Chaplain General*,
    1960, p.157.
6. James Watson, interview with author, 10 August 1986.
7. Gladden, opus cit.
8. Ibid.
9. Major General Frank Richardson CB DSO OBE MD, medical postscript in a study
    of Capital Courts Martial, 1914–18, *For the Sake of Example* by His Honour Judge
    Anthony Babington, pp.220/223. Leo Cooper, London, 1983.
10. Studdert Kennedy.
11. Vallings, in Hardy, ibid
12. Sheringham, in Hardy, ibid.
13. Studdert Kennedy, *To Stretcher Bearers*, ibid.

Chapter 13

1. Sheringham, letter to Mary Hardy.
2. *Carlisle Diocesan Gazette*, November 1918.
3. Vallings.
4. Hitch.
5. Hitch.
6. Vallings.
7. *Carlisle Diocesan Gazette*, ibid.
8. Wyrall, opus cit.
9. Ibid.
10. Ibid.
11. Calvert, ibid.
12. Carey, ibid.
13. Sheringham, ibid.
14. Hitch, ibid.
15. The Reverend Theodore Bayley Hardy is buried in the Military Cemetery, St. Sever
    Extension, Rouen, France. Block S, Plot V, Row J, Grave 1.

Index

Abbott, Rev Dr Edwin, 11–12, 16
Adams, A.W., 21
Asquith, Rt Hon Herbert Henry, MP, 6–7, 9, 77
Athanasian Creed, 3, 25

Ball, Albert VC DSO MC, 23
Birkbech, George, 7
Brougham, Henry, 7,
Brown Capt F., 62
Bruce-Williams, Maj-Gen Sir Hugh, 64–5, 107–108
Byron, Lord George Gordon, 16

Calvert, Pte Maurice, 139
Carey, Rev Douglas, 44, 47, 49–52, 140
Challenor, Lt. Col., 92
Cubitt, Gen Sir Thomas Astley, CMG, DSO, 75–6
Cuffley, Robert, 4–5,

Dickens, Charles, 2, 5–6
Driscoll, Jimmy, 50

Gow, Rev Dr James, 15–18, 21
Graves, Robert, 46, 64
Gwynne, Bishop Llewellyn Henry CMG CBE, 26, 41, 44, 115

Hacker, Bishop George, 117
Hardy, Alfred, 1–3
Hardy, Bessie, 34–5
Hardy, Elizabeth (daughter), 2, 21, 28, 33, 39–40, 66, 111–13, 115–16, 140
Hardy, Florence Elizabeth, nee Hastings, 13, 20, 33–4
Hardy, George, 1–2
Hardy, Ernest, 1, 3, 6, 12
Hardy, Mary, 6, 12, 25, 35, 50, 55, 115–16, 121, 141

Hardy, Robert, 1
Hardy, Dr William (son), 28, 33–4, 38–40, 66–7, 110, 115
Hastings-Hardy, Patricia, 116, 127, 142
Hardy, Sarah Richards, 1, 3–4, 7
Hardyman, Lt. Col John Hay Maitland DSO MC, 55–60, 83, 114–15
Hastings, William, 13, 20
Heath, Rev Charles, 9, 12
Hitch, Lt. Col Arthur Tyler DSO, 68–70, 98, 136, 141, 143
Huntley, Henry, 1
Huntley, Georgina, 4

Lawrence, David Herbert, 17, 22
Llewellyn, John, 31

Macdonald, Ramsay, 58–9
Madden, Lt C.R. MC, 65
Martin, Bernard, 46–7, 63
Montague, Charles, 9–11, 45
Moore, George, 2, 5
Morel, Edmund Dene, 59
Mortimer, Rev Dr G.F., 8
Mott, Fred Sergeant, 113–14

O'Connor, Feargus, 16
Owen Wilfred, 42

Ponsonby, Arthur, 59

Radford, Sgt George, DCM, 106–107
Ridding, Rev. Dr George, 17, 25, 27–8
Russell, Bertrand, 59

Sage, Pte Thomas, VC, 95–6
Sassoon, Siegfried, 45, 80
Scott, C.P., 10
Scott, Lt. Col John Willoughby DSO, 55–8, 83

Sheringham, Lt. Col, 130, 137
St Albans, Duke of, 17
Studdertt Kennedy, Rev Geoffrey MC, 21, 47–54, 123

Thompson, Rev Reginald, 27
Trevelyan, Charles Philips, 59

Vallings, Rev Geoffrey, DSO, 65–6, 80, 82–3, 96–7, 118, 132

von Richthofen, Frieda, 22
von Richthofen, Baron Manfred, 22–3

Ward, Rev Reginald, 27
Watson, Pte Jimmy, 64, 90, 100, 120, 138
Westrop, Canon Michael, 116
Wilkinson, William John Playter, 2
Wilson, Jonty, 36–8

Yaw, Sgt Maj DCM, 98–100, 109